Essentials of Business Communication

Seventh Edition

Mary Ellen Guffey

THOMSON
™
SOUTH-WESTERN

Australia · Canada · Mexico · Singapore · Spain · United Kingdom · United States

Essentials of Business Communication, Seventh Edition
Mary Ellen Guffey

Executive Editors:
Michele Baird, Maureen Staudt &
Michael Stranz

Project Development Manager:
Linda de Stefano

Marketing Coordinators:
Lindsay Annett and Sara Mercurio

Production/Manufacturing Supervisor:
Donna M. Brown

Pre-Media Services Supervisor:
Dan Plofchan

Rights and Permissions Specialists:
Kalina Hintz and Bahman Naraghi

Cover Image
Getty Images*

The Adaptable Courseware Program consists of products and additions to existing Thomson products that are produced from camera-ready copy. Peer review, class testing, and accuracy are primarily the responsibility of the author(s).

ISBN 0-324-37230-2

International Divisions List

Asia (Including India):
Thomson Learning
(a division of Thomson Asia Pte Ltd)
5 Shenton Way #01-01
UIC Building
Singapore 068808
Tel: (65) 6410-1200
Fax: (65) 6410-1208

Australia/New Zealand:
Thomson Learning Australia
102 Dodds Street
Southbank, Victoria 3006
Australia

Latin America:
Thomson Learning
Seneca 53
Colonia Polano
11560 Mexico, D.F., Mexico
Tel (525) 281-2906
Fax (525) 281-2656

Canada:
Thomson Nelson
1120 Birchmount Road
Toronto, Ontario
Canada M1K 5G4
Tel (416) 752-9100
Fax (416) 752-8102

UK/Europe/Middle East/Africa:
Thomson Learning
High Holborn House
50-51 Bedford Row
London, WC1R 4LS
United Kingdom
Tel 44 (020) 7067-2500
Fax 44 (020) 7067-2600

Spain (Includes Portugal):
Thomson Paraninfo
Calle Magallanes 25
28015 Madrid
España
Tel 34 (0)91 446-3350
Fax 34 (0)91 445-6218

Contents

CHAPTER 1

BUILDING YOUR CAREER SUCCESS WITH COMMUNICATION SKILLS

> " *If I went back to college again, I'd concentrate on two areas: learning to write and to speak before an audience. Nothing in life is more important than the ability to communicate effectively.* "
>
> **Gerald R. Ford**, 38th President of the United States

OBJECTIVES

- Understand the importance of becoming an effective and professional communicator in today's changing workplace.

- Examine the process of communication.

- Discuss how to become an effective listener.

- Analyze nonverbal communication and explain techniques for improving nonverbal communication skills.

- Explain how culture affects communication, and describe methods for improving cross-cultural communication.

- Identify specific techniques that improve effective communication among diverse workplace audiences.

THE IMPORTANCE OF COMMUNICATION SKILLS TO YOUR CAREER

Three decades ago when he was president, Gerald Ford spoke about the importance of communication skills. If he had a second chance at college, he said, he'd concentrate on learning to write and learning to speak. Today, communication is even more important and more challenging than in President Ford's time. We live in an information age that revolves around communication.

Communication skills are critical to your job placement, performance, career advancement, and organizational success.

Developing excellent communication skills is extremely important to your future career. Surveys of employers often show that communication skills are critical to effective job placement, performance, career advancement, and organizational success.[1] In making hiring decisions, employers often rank communication skills among the most requested competencies. Many job advertisements specifically ask for excellent oral and written communication skills. In a poll of recruiters, oral and written communication skills were by a large margin the top skill set sought in applicants.[2] Another survey of managers and executives ranked the skills most lacking in job candidates, and writing skills topped that list.[3]

Communication skills consistently rank near the top of competencies sought by recruiters. Because more and more messages are being sent, writing skills are particularly important to succeed in first jobs and to be promoted into management.

Writing Skills and Professionalism Lead to Success

Advancements in technology mean that writing skills are increasingly important because more messages are being exchanged.

Writing skills are particularly important today because technological advances enable us to transmit messages more rapidly, more often, and to greater numbers of people than ever before. Writing skills, which were always a career advantage, are now a necessity.[4] They can be your ticket to work—or your ticket out the door, according to a business executive responding to a recent survey. This survey of 120 American corporations, by the National Commission on Writing, a panel established by the College Board, found that two thirds of salaried employees have some writing responsibility. Yet, about one third of them do not meet the writing requirements for their positions.[5]

"Businesses are crying out—they need to have people who write better," said Gaston Caperton, executive and College Board president. The ability to write opens doors to professional employment. People who cannot write and communicate clearly will not be hired. If already working, they are unlikely to last long enough to be considered for promotion.

Writing is a marker of high-skill, high-wage, professional work, according to Bob Kerrey, president of New School University in New York and chair of the National Commission on Writing. If you can't express yourself clearly, he says, you limit your opportunities for salaried positions.[6] But writing skills are also important for non-salaried workers such as electricians, engineers, technicians, and supervisors, who must create reports for government agencies and regulatory bodies. Even hourly workers must be able to communicate to exchange messages.

Businesses don't want spellbinding storytellers; they want people who can write clearly and concisely.

Lamenting the sorry state of business writing skills, a front-page article in *The New York Times* announced, "What Corporate America Can't Build: A Sentence." Quoted in the article, Susan Traiman, a director of the Business Roundtable, an association of leading chief executives, said, "It's not that companies want to hire Tolstoy."[7] They aren't seeking spellbinding authors; they just want people who can write clearly and concisely. Because so many lack these skills, businesses are spending as much as $3.1 billion annually on remedial training.

In addition to expecting employees to write clearly, businesses expect employees to act in a businesslike and professional manner on the job. Some new-hires have no idea that excessive absenteeism or tardiness are grounds for termination. Others are surprised to learn that they are expected to devote their full attention to their duties when on the job. One young man wanted to read Harry Potter novels when things got slow. Even more employees don't realize that they are sabotaging their careers when they sprinkle their conversation with *like*, *you know*, and uptalk (making declarative statements sound like questions). Companies are reluctant to promote people into management who do not look or sound credible. Figure 1.1 reviews six areas you will want to check to be sure you are not sending the wrong message with unwitting or unprofessional behavior.

FIGURE 1.1

Projecting Professionalism When You Communicate

	Unprofessional	Professional
Speech habits	Speaking in *uptalk*, a singsong speech pattern that has a rising inflection making sentences sound like questions. Using *like* to fill in mindless chatter, substituting *go* for *said*, relying on slang, or letting profanity slip into your conversation.	Recognizing that your credibility can be seriously damaged by sounding uneducated, crude, or like a teenager.
E-mail	Writing messages with incomplete sentences, misspelled words, exclamation points, IM slang, and mindless chatting. Sloppy, careless messages send a nonverbal message that you don't care, don't know, or aren't smart enough to know what is correct.	Employers like to see subjects, verbs, and punctuation marks. They don't recognize IM abbreviations. Call it crazy, but they value conciseness and correct spelling, even in brief e-mail messages.
Internet	Using an e-mail address such as *hotbabe@hotmail.com*, *supasnugglykitty.yahoo.com*, or *buffedguy@aol.com*.	An e-mail address that is your name or a relevant, positive, businesslike expression. It should not sound cute or like a chat room nickname.
Answering machine/ voice mail	An outgoing message with strident background music, weird sounds, or a joke message.	An outgoing message that states your name or phone number and provides instructions for leaving a message.
Telephone	Soap operas, thunderous music, or a TV football game playing noisily in the background when you answer the phone.	A quiet background when you answer the telephone, especially if you are expecting a prospective employer's call.
Cell phone	Taking or placing cell phone calls during business meetings or during conversations with fellow employees. Raising your voice (cell yell) or engaging in cell calls when others must reluctantly overhear.	Never letting a cell phone interrupt business meetings. Using your cell only when conversations can be private.

Using This Book to Build Career Communication Skills

Because communication skills are learned, you control how well you communicate.

This book focuses on developing basic writing skills. You will, however, also learn to improve your listening, nonverbal, and speaking skills. The abilities to read, listen, speak, and write effectively, of course, are not inborn. When it comes to communication, it's more *nurture* than *nature*. Good communicators are not born; they are made. Thriving in the dynamic and demanding new world of work will depend on many factors, some of which you cannot control. One factor that you *do* control, however, is how well you communicate.

Developing career-boosting communication skills requires instruction, practice, and feedback from a specialist.

The goal of this book is to teach you basic business communication skills. These include learning how to write an e-mail, letter, or report and how to make a presentation. Anyone can learn these skills with the help of instructional materials and good model documents, all of which you'll find in this book. You also need practice—with meaningful feedback. You need someone such as your instructor to tell you how to modify your responses so that you can improve.

We've designed this book, its supplements, and two Web sites (*http://guffeyxtra .swlearning.com* and *http://guffey.swlearning.com*) to provide you and your instructor with everything necessary to make you a successful business communicator in today's dynamic but demanding workplace. Given the increasing emphasis on communication, many businesses are paying huge sums to communication coaches and trainers to teach employees the very skills that you are learning in this course. Your coach is your instructor. So, get your money's worth! Pick your instructor's brains.

This book and this course might well be the most important in your entire college career.

With this book as your guide and your instructor as your coach, you may find this course to be the most important in your entire college curriculum. To get started, this first chapter presents an overview. You'll take a quick look at the changing workplace, the communication process, listening, nonverbal communication, culture and communication, and workplace diversity. The remainder of the book is devoted to developing specific writing and speaking skills.

Succeeding in the Changing World of Work

Trends in the new world of work emphasize the importance of communication skills.

The world of work is changing dramatically. The kind of work you'll do, the tools you'll use, the form of management you'll work under, the environment in which you'll work, the people with whom you'll interact—all are undergoing a pronounced transformation. Many of the changes in this dynamic workplace revolve around processing and communicating information. As a result, the most successful players in this new world of work will be those with highly developed communication skills. The following business trends illustrate the importance of excellent communication skills.

- **Flattened management hierarchies.** To better compete and to reduce expenses, businesses have for years been trimming layers of management. This means that as a frontline employee, you will have fewer managers. You will be making decisions and communicating them to customers, to fellow employees, and to executives.

Today's employees must contribute to improving productivity and profitability.

- **More participatory management.** Gone are the days of command-and-control management. Now, even new employees like you will be expected to understand and contribute to the big picture. Improving productivity and profitability will be everyone's job, not just management's.

- **Increased emphasis on self-directed work groups and virtual teams.** Businesses today are often run by cross-functional teams of peers. You can expect to work with a team in gathering information, finding and sharing solutions, implementing decisions, and managing conflict. You may even become part of a virtual team whose members are in remote locations and who communicate almost exclusively electronically. Good communication skills are extremely important in working together successfully in all team environments, especially if members do not meet face-to-face.

FIGURE 1.2

Communication
Technologies

Reshaping the World of Work

Today's workplace is changing dramatically as a result of innovative software, superfast wireless networks, and numerous technologies that allow workers to share information, work from remote locations, and be more efficient and productive in or away from the office. We're seeing a gradual progression from basic capabilities, such as e-mail and calendaring, to deeper functionality, such as remote database access and worldwide videoconferencing. Becoming familiar with modern workplace and collaboration technologies can help you be successful in today's digital workplace.

IP Telephony: VoIP

Savvy businesses are switching from traditional phone service to Voice over Internet Protocol (VoIP). This technology allows callers to make telephone calls using a broadband Internet connection, thus eliminating long-distance and local telephone charges.

Wireless Networks and Wi-Fi

No longer are computers and workers chained to their desks. Wireless networks use radio waves to send signals and connect to the Internet. Combined with high-speed broadband connections, these networks have fueled the increasing use of laptop computers and portable devices. Public Wi-Fi (Wireless Fidelity) "hot spots" provide free connections that further expand the range of laptops, PDAs (personal digital assistants), and handheld devices such as the BlackBerry and the Treo. Wireless networks enable business communicators to work anywhere, anytime, and still remain connected to office e-mail, company files, and programs such as Word and Excel.

Company Intranets

To share insider information, many companies provide their own protected Web site called an intranet. It may handle company e-mail, announcements, an employee directory, a policy handbook, frequently asked questions, personnel forms and data, employee discussion forums, shared documents, and other employee information.

Electronic Presentations

Business presenters load a slide presentation onto a laptop PC or PDA for handy electronic presentations in rooms equipped with projectors. Sophisticated presentations may include animations, sound effects, digital photos, video clips, or even hyperlinks to Internet sites.

Voice Recognition

Computers equipped with voice recognition software enable users to dictate up to 160 words a minute with accurate transcription. Voice recognition is particularly helpful to disabled workers and to professionals with heavy dictation loads, such as physicians and attorneys. Users can create documents, enter data, compose and send e-mails, browse the Web, and control the desktop—all by voice.

Global competition, expanding markets, and the ever-increasing pace of business accelerate the development of exciting collaboration tools. Employees working together may be down the hall, across the country, or around the world. With today's tools, workers exchange ideas, solve problems, develop products, forecast future performance, and complete team projects any time of the day or night and anywhere in the world.

Voice Conferencing

Telephone "bridges" join two or more callers from any location to share the same call. Voice conferencing (also called audioconferencing, teleconferencing, or just plain conference calling) enables people to collaborate by telephone. Communicators at both ends use an enhanced speakerphone to talk and be heard simultaneously.

Web Conferencing

With services such as WebEx and Live Meeting, all you need are a PC and an Internet connection to hold a meeting. Although the functions of Web conferencing (also called desktop or media conferencing) are constantly evolving, it currently incorporates screen sharing, voice communication, slide presentations, text messaging, and application sharing (e.g., participants can work on a spreadsheet together).

Videoconferencing

Videoconferencing allows participants to meet in special conference rooms equipped with cameras and television screens. Groups see each other and interact in real time although they may be worlds apart. Faster computers, rapid Internet connections, and better cameras now enable 2 to 200 participants to sit at their own PCs and share applications, spreadsheets, presentations, and photos.

Video Phones

Using advanced video compression technology, video phones transmit real-time audio and video so that communicators can see

each other as they collaborate. With a video phone, you can videoconference without a computer or a television screen.

One-Number Dialing

Smart phones switch seamlessly between cellular networks and corporate Wi-Fi connections allowing employees to take their phones around corporate campuses, into their homes, or on the road. One-number dialing reduces frustration and wasted time.

Presence Technology

Responding to the demand for immediate communication, "presence awareness" builds on instant messaging. In a presence-enabled workplace, you would know whether to contact someone via voice, e-mail, or instant messaging. This awareness avoids time wasted in voice mailboxes and waiting for e-mail responses. A light on your telephone might indicate when key people on your team are present on your internal phone network. Still being developed, presence technology is built on Session Initiation Protocol (SIP).

Increasing global competition and revolutionary technologies demand cultural and communication skills.

- **Heightened global competition.** Because American companies are moving beyond local markets, you may be interacting with people from many different cultures. As a successful business communicator, you will want to learn about other cultures. You'll also need to develop multicultural skills including sensitivity, flexibility, patience, and tolerance.

- **Innovative communication technologies.** E-mail, fax, instant messaging, text messaging, the Web, mobile technologies, audio- and videoconferencing, company intranets, and voice recognition—all these innovative technologies are reshaping the way we communicate at work, as summarized in Figure 1.2. You can expect to be communicating more often and more rapidly than ever before. Your writing and speaking skills will be showcased as never before.

- **New work environments.** Mobile technologies and the desire for a better balance between work and family have resulted in flexible working arrangements. You may become part of an increasing number of workers who are telecommuters or virtual team members. Working as a telecommuter or virtual team member requires even more communication, because staying connected with the office or with one another means exchanging many messages. Another work environment trend is the movement toward open offices divided into small work cubicles. Working in a cubicle requires new rules of office etiquette and civility.

- **Focus on information and knowledge as corporate assets.** Corporate America is increasingly aware that information is the key to better products and increased profitability. You will be expected to gather, sort, store, and disseminate data in a timely and accurate fashion. This is the new way of business life.

EXAMINING THE COMMUNICATION PROCESS

As you can see, you can expect to be communicating more rapidly, more often, and with greater numbers of people than ever before. The most successful players in this new world of work will be those with highly developed communication skills. Because good communication skills are essential to your success, we need to take a closer look at the communication process.

Communication is the transmission of information and meaning from one individual or group to another.

Just what is communication? For our purposes *communication is the transmission of information and meaning from one individual or group to another.* The crucial element in this definition is *meaning.* Communication has as its central objective the transmission of meaning. The process of communication is successful only when the receiver understands an idea as the sender intended it. This process generally involves five steps, discussed here and shown in Figure 1.3.

1. **Sender has an idea.** The form of the idea may be influenced by the sender's mood, frame of reference, background, culture, and physical makeup, as well as the context of the situation.

2. **Sender encodes the idea in a message.** *Encoding* means converting the idea into words or gestures that will convey meaning. A major problem in communicating any message verbally is that words have different meanings for different people. That's why skilled communicators try to choose familiar words with concrete meanings on which both senders and receivers agree.

The communication process has five steps: idea formation, message encoding, message transmission, message decoding, and feedback.

3. **Message travels over a channel.** The medium over which the message is transmitted is the *channel.* Messages may be sent by computer, telephone, letter, or memorandum. They may also be sent by means of a report, announcement, picture, spoken word, fax, or other channel. Because both verbal and nonverbal messages are carried, senders must choose channels carefully. Anything that disrupts the transmission of a message in the communication process is called *noise.*

FIGURE 1.3   **Communication Process**

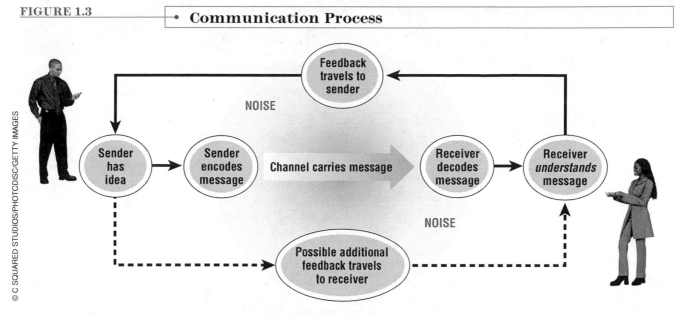

Communication barriers and noise may cause the communication process to break down.

Channel noise ranges from static that disrupts a telephone conversation to spelling errors in an e-mail message. Such errors damage the credibility of the sender.

4. **Receiver decodes message.** The person for whom a message is intended is the *receiver*. Translating the message from its symbol form into meaning involves *decoding*. Successful communication takes place only when a receiver understands the meaning intended by the sender. Such success is often hard to achieve because no two people share the same background. Success is further limited because barriers and noise may disrupt the process.

5. **Feedback travels to sender.** The verbal and nonverbal responses of the receiver create *feedback*, a vital part of the entire communication process. Feedback helps the sender know that the message was received and understood. Senders can encourage feedback by asking questions such as *Am I making myself clear?* and *Is there anything you don't understand?* Senders can further improve feedback by delivering the message at a time when receivers can respond. Senders should provide only as much information as a receiver can handle. Receivers can improve the process by paraphrasing the sender's message. They might say, *Let me try to explain that in my own words,* or *My understanding of your comment is . . .*

DEVELOPING BETTER LISTENING SKILLS

An important part of the communication process is listening. By all accounts, however, most of us are not very good listeners. Do you ever pretend to be listening when you're not? Do you know how to look attentive in class when your mind wanders far away? How about "tuning out" people when their ideas are boring or complex? Do you find it hard to focus on ideas when a speaker's clothing or mannerisms are unusual?

You probably answered *yes* to one or more of these questions because many of us have developed poor listening habits. In fact, some researchers suggest that we listen at only 25 percent efficiency. Such poor listening habits are costly in business. Letters must be rewritten, shipments reshipped, appointments rescheduled, contracts renegotiated, and directions restated.

Most individuals listen at only 25 percent efficiency.

© C SQUARED STUDIOS/PHOTODISC/GETTY IMAGES

© Ted Goff (www.tedgoff.com)

COMMUNICATION TOOLS

GOFF

Observers have suggested that the best communication tools are ears.

Most North Americans speak at about 125 words per minute. The human brain can process information at least three times as fast.

To improve listening skills, we must first recognize barriers that prevent effective listening. Then we need to focus on specific techniques that are effective in improving listening skills.

Barriers to Effective Listening

As you learned earlier, barriers and noise can interfere with the communication process. Have any of the following barriers and distractions prevented you from hearing what's said?

- **Physical barriers.** You cannot listen if you cannot hear what is being said. Physical impediments include hearing disabilities, poor acoustics, and noisy surroundings. It's also difficult to listen if you're ill, tired, uncomfortable, or worried.
- **Psychological barriers.** Everyone brings to the communication process a different set of cultural, ethical, and personal values. Each of us has an idea of what is right and what is important. If other ideas run counter to our preconceived thoughts, we tend to "tune out" the speaker and thus fail to hear.
- **Language problems.** Unfamiliar words can destroy the communication process because they lack meaning for the receiver. In addition, emotion-laden or "charged" words can adversely affect listening. If the mention of words such as *abortion* or *overdose* has an intense emotional impact, a listener may be unable to think about the words that follow.
- **Nonverbal distractions.** Many of us find it hard to listen if a speaker is different from what we view as normal. Unusual clothing, speech mannerisms, body twitches, or a radical hairstyle can cause enough distraction to prevent us from hearing what the speaker has to say.
- **Thought speed.** Because we can process thoughts more than three times faster than speakers can say them, we can become bored and allow our minds to wander.

The better a business-person listens to a customer, the better she or he will be at fulfilling expectations, resolving disputes, reducing uncertainty, and projecting goodwill. Any employee listening to a customer should learn to defer judgment, pay attention to content rather than surface issues, focus on main ideas, and avoid replying to sidetracking issues.

- **Faking attention.** Most of us have learned to look as if we are listening even when we're not. Such behavior was perhaps necessary as part of our socialization. Faked attention, however, seriously threatens effective listening because it encourages the mind to engage in flights of unchecked fancy. Those who practice faked attention often find it hard to concentrate even when they want to.
- **Grandstanding.** Would you rather talk or listen? Naturally, most of us would rather talk. Because our own experiences and thoughts are most important to us, we grab the limelight in conversations. We sometimes fail to listen carefully because we're just waiting politely for the next pause so that we can have our turn to speak.

Tips for Becoming an Active Listener

You can reverse the harmful effects of poor habits by making a conscious effort to become an active listener. This means becoming involved. You can't sit back and hear whatever a lazy mind happens to receive. The following techniques will help you become an active and effective listener.

To become an active listener, stop talking, control your surroundings, develop a positive mind-set, listen for main points, and capitalize on lag time.

- **Stop talking.** The first step to becoming a good listener is to stop talking. Let others explain their views. Learn to concentrate on what the speaker is saying, not on what your next comment will be.
- **Control your surroundings.** Whenever possible, remove competing sounds. Close windows or doors, turn off TVs, unplug your iPod, and move away from loud people, noisy appliances, or engines. Choose a quiet time and place for listening.

© Ted Goff (www.tedgoff.com)

"How can I listen to you if you don't say the things I want to hear?"

- **Establish a receptive mind-set.** Expect to learn something by listening. Strive for a positive and receptive frame of mind. If the message is complex, think of it as mental gymnastics. It's hard work but good exercise to stretch and expand the limits of your mind.
- **Keep an open mind.** We all sift and filter information through our own biases and values. For improved listening, discipline yourself to listen objectively. Be fair to the speaker. Hear what is really being said, not what you want to hear.
- **Listen for main points.** Heighten your concentration and satisfaction by looking for the speaker's central themes. Congratulate yourself when you find them!
- **Capitalize on lag time.** Make use of the quickness of your mind by reviewing the speaker's points. Anticipate what's coming next. Evaluate evidence the speaker has presented. Don't allow yourself to daydream. Try to guess what the speaker's next point will be.
- **Listen between the lines.** Focus both on what is spoken as well as what is unspoken. Listen for feelings as well as for facts.
- **Judge ideas, not appearances.** Concentrate on the content of the message, not on its delivery. Avoid being distracted by the speaker's looks, voice, or mannerisms.
- **Hold your fire.** Force yourself to listen to the speaker's entire argument or message before reacting. Such restraint may enable you to understand the speaker's reasons and logic before you jump to false conclusions.
- **Take selective notes.** In some situations thoughtful notetaking may be necessary to record important facts that must be recalled later. Select only the most important points so that the notetaking process does not interfere with your concentration on the speaker's total message.

Listening actively may mean taking notes and providing feedback.

- **Provide feedback.** Let the speaker know that you are listening. Nod your head and maintain eye contact. Ask relevant questions at appropriate times. Getting involved improves the communication process for both the speaker and the listener.

IMPROVING YOUR NONVERBAL COMMUNICATION SKILLS

Understanding messages often involves more than merely listening to spoken words. Nonverbal cues, in fact, can speak louder than words. These cues include eye contact, facial expression, body movements, space, time, territory, and appearance. All these nonverbal cues affect how a message is interpreted, or decoded, by the receiver.

Nonverbal communication includes all unwritten and unspoken messages, intended or not.

Just what is nonverbal communication? It includes all unwritten and unspoken messages, whether intended or not. These silent signals have a strong effect on receivers. But understanding them is not simple. Does a downward glance indicate modesty? Fatigue? Does a constant stare reflect coldness? Dullness? Do crossed arms mean defensiveness? Withdrawal? Or do crossed arms just mean that a person is shivering?

Messages are even harder to decipher when the verbal codes and nonverbal cues do not agree. What will you think if Scott says he's not angry, but he slams the door when he leaves? What if Alicia assures the hostess that the meal is excellent, but she eats very little? The nonverbal messages in these situations speak more loudly than the words.

When verbal and nonverbal messages clash, listeners tend to believe the nonverbal message.

When verbal and nonverbal messages conflict, receivers put more faith in nonverbal cues. In one study speakers sent a positive message but averted their eyes as they spoke. Listeners perceived the total message to be negative. Moreover, they thought that averted eyes suggested lack of affection, superficiality, lack of trust, and nonreceptivity.[8]

Successful communicators recognize the power of nonverbal messages. Although it's unwise to attach specific meanings to gestures or actions, some cues broadcast by body language are helpful in understanding the feelings and attitudes of senders.

How the Eyes, Face, and Body Send Silent Messages

Words seldom tell the whole story. Indeed, some messages are sent with no words at all. The eyes, face, and body can convey a world of meaning without a single syllable being spoken.

EYE CONTACT

The eyes are thought to be the best predictor of a speaker's true feelings.

The eyes have been called the *windows to the soul.* Even if they don't reveal the soul, the eyes are often the best predictor of a speaker's true feelings. Most of us cannot look another person straight in the eyes and lie. As a result, in American culture we tend to believe people who look directly at us. Sustained eye contact suggests trust and admiration; brief eye contact signals fear or stress. Good eye contact enables the message sender to see whether a receiver is paying attention, showing respect, responding favorably, or feeling distress. From the receiver's viewpoint, good eye contact, in North American culture, reveals the speaker's sincerity, confidence, and truthfulness.

FACIAL EXPRESSION

The expression on a person's face can be almost as revealing of emotion as the eyes. Experts estimate that the human face can display over 250,000 expressions.[9] To hide their feelings, some people can control these expressions and maintain "poker faces." Most of us, however, display our emotions openly. Raising or lowering the eyebrows, squinting the eyes, swallowing nervously, clenching the jaw, smiling broadly—these voluntary and involuntary facial expressions can add to or entirely replace verbal messages.

© Ted Goff (www.tedgoff.com)

"I know you're saying no, but I think your body language is saying maybe."

POSTURE AND GESTURES

A person's posture can convey anything from high status and self-confidence to shyness and submissiveness. Leaning toward a speaker suggests attraction and interest; pulling away or shrinking back denotes fear, distrust, anxiety, or disgust. Similarly, gestures can communicate entire thoughts via simple movements. However, the meanings of some of these movements differ in other cultures. Unless you know local customs, they can get you into trouble. In the United States and Canada, for example, forming the thumb and forefinger in a circle means everything's OK. But in Germany and parts of South America, the OK sign is obscene.

What does your own body language say about you? To take stock of the kinds of messages being sent by your body, ask a classmate to critique your use of eye contact, facial expression, and body movements. Another way to analyze your nonverbal style is to videotape yourself making a presentation. Then study your performance. This way you can make sure your nonverbal cues send the same message as your words.

Nonverbal messages often have different meanings in different cultures.

How Time, Space, and Territory Send Silent Messages

In addition to nonverbal messages transmitted by your body, three external elements convey information in the communication process: time, space, and territory.

"Sorry, Ridgely, but this area is my personal space."

© ScienceCartoonsPlus.com

TIME

How we structure and use time tells observers about our personality and attitudes. For example, when Donald Trump, multimillionaire real estate developer, gives a visitor a prolonged interview, he signals his respect for, interest in, and approval of the visitor or the topic to be discussed.

SPACE

How we order the space around us tells something about ourselves and our objectives. Whether the space is a bedroom, a dorm room, an office, or a department, people reveal themselves in the design and grouping of their furniture. Generally, the more formal the arrangement, the more formal and closed the communication. The way office furniture is arranged sends cues on how communication is to take place. Former FBI director J. Edgar Hoover used to make his visitors sit at a small table below his large, elevated desk. Clearly, he did not want office visitors to feel equal to him.[10]

TERRITORY

Each of us has a certain area that we feel is our own territory, whether it's a specific spot or just the space around us. Your father may have a favorite chair in which he is most comfortable, a cook might not tolerate intruders in his or her kitchen, and veteran employees may feel that certain work areas and tools belong to them. We all maintain zones of privacy in which we feel comfortable. Figure 1.4 illustrates the four zones of social interaction among Americans, as formulated by anthropologist Edward T. Hall.[11] Notice that Americans are a bit standoffish; only intimate friends and family may stand closer than about 1½ feet. If someone violates that territory, Americans feel uncomfortable and defensive and may step back to reestablish their space.

People convey meaning in how they structure and organize time and how they order the space around themselves.

How Appearance Sends Silent Messages

The physical appearance of a business document, as well as the personal appearance of an individual, transmits immediate and important nonverbal messages.

FIGURE 1.4

> **Four Space Zones for Social Interaction**

| **Intimate Zone** (1 to 1½ feet) | **Personal Zone** (1½ to 4 feet) | **Social Zone** (4 to 12 feet) | **Public Zone** (12 or more feet) |

APPEARANCE OF BUSINESS DOCUMENTS

The appearance of a message and of an individual can convey positive or negative nonverbal messages.

The way a letter, memo, or report looks can have either a positive or a negative effect on the receiver. Sloppy e-mail messages send a nonverbal message that says you are in a terrific hurry or that the receiver is not important enough for you to care. Envelopes—through their postage, stationery, and printing—can suggest routine, important, or junk mail. Letters and reports can look neat, professional, well organized, and attractive—or just the opposite. In succeeding chapters you'll learn how to create documents that send positive nonverbal messages through their appearance, format, organization, readability, and correctness.

PERSONAL APPEARANCE

The way you look—your clothing, grooming, and posture—telegraphs an instant nonverbal message about you. Based on what they see, viewers make quick judgments about your status, credibility, personality, and potential. If you want to be considered professional, think about how you present yourself. One marketing manager said, "I'm young and pretty. It's hard enough to be taken seriously, and if I show up in jeans and a T-shirt, I don't stand a chance."[12] As a businessperson, you'll want to think about what your appearance says about you. Although the rules of business attire have loosened up, some workers show poor judgment. You'll learn more about professional attire and behavior in later chapters.

Tips for Improving Your Nonverbal Skills

Because nonverbal cues can mean more than spoken words, learn to use nonverbal communication positively.

Nonverbal communication can outweigh words in the way it influences how others perceive us. You can harness the power of silent messages by reviewing the following tips for improving nonverbal communication skills:

- **Establish and maintain eye contact.** Remember that in the United States and Canada, appropriate eye contact signals interest, attentiveness, strength, and credibility.
- **Use posture to show interest.** Encourage communication interaction by leaning forward, sitting or standing erect, and looking alert.
- **Improve your decoding skills.** Watch facial expressions and body language to understand the complete verbal and nonverbal messages being communicated.
- **Probe for more information.** When you perceive nonverbal cues that contradict verbal meanings, politely seek additional cues (*I'm not sure I understand, Please tell me more about . . . ,* or *Do you mean that . . .*).
- **Avoid assigning nonverbal meanings out of context.** Don't interpret nonverbal behavior unless you understand a situation or a culture.
- **Associate with people from diverse cultures.** Learn about other cultures to widen your knowledge and tolerance of intercultural nonverbal messages.

- **Appreciate the power of appearance.** Keep in mind that the appearance of your business documents, your business space, and yourself sends immediate positive or negative messages to receivers.
- **Observe yourself on videotape.** Ensure that your verbal and nonverbal messages are in sync by taping and evaluating yourself making a presentation.
- **Enlist friends and family.** Ask them to monitor your conscious and unconscious body movements and gestures to help you become a more effective communicator.

UNDERSTANDING HOW CULTURE AFFECTS COMMUNICATION

Verbal and nonverbal meanings are even more difficult to interpret when people are from different cultures.

Comprehending the verbal and nonverbal meanings of a message is difficult even when communicators are from the same culture. But when they are from different cultures, special sensitivity and skills are necessary.

Negotiators for a North American company learned this lesson when they were in Japan looking for a trading partner. The North Americans were pleased after their first meeting with representatives of a major Japanese firm. The Japanese had nodded assent throughout the meeting and had not objected to a single proposal. The next day, however, the North Americans were stunned to learn that the Japanese had rejected the entire plan. In interpreting the nonverbal behavioral messages, the North Americans made a typical mistake. They assumed the Japanese were nodding in agreement as fellow North Americans would. In this case, however, the nods of assent indicated comprehension—not approval.

Every country has a unique culture or common heritage, joint experience, and shared learning that produce its culture. Their common experience gives members of that culture a complex system of shared values and customs. It teaches them how to behave; it conditions their reactions. Global business, new communication technologies, the Internet, and even Hollywood are spreading Western values throughout the world. Yet, cultural differences can still cause significant misunderstandings.

Comparing traditional North American values with those in other cultures will broaden your worldview. This comparison should also help you recognize some of the values that influence your actions and affect your opinions of others.

Comparing Key Cultural Values

Until relatively recently, typical North Americans shared the same broad cultural values. Some experts identified them as "Anglo" or "mainstream" values.[13] These values largely represented white, male, Northern European views. Women and many minorities now entering the workforce may eventually modify these values. However, a majority of North Americans are still governed by these mainstream values.

Although North American culture is complex, we'll focus on four dimensions to help you better understand some of the values that shape your actions and judgments of others. These four dimensions are individualism, formality, communication style, and time orientation.

INDIVIDUALISM

While North Americans value individualism and personal responsibility, other cultures emphasize group- and team-oriented values.

One of the most identifiable characteristics of North Americans is their *individualism*. This is an attitude of independence and freedom from control. They think that initiative and self-assertion result in personal achievement. They believe in individual action, self-reliance, and personal responsibility; and they desire a large degree of freedom in their personal lives. Other cultures emphasize membership in organizations, groups, and teams; they encourage acceptance of group values, duties, and decisions. Members of these cultures typically resist independence because it fosters competition and confrontation instead of consensus.

FORMALITY

Although North Americans value informality and directness, other cultures may value tradition and indirectness.

A second significant dimension of North American culture is our attitude toward *formality*. Americans place less emphasis on tradition, ceremony, and social rules than do people in some other cultures. They dress casually and are soon on a first-name basis with others. Their lack of formality is often characterized by directness. In business dealings North Americans tend to come to the point immediately; indirectness, they feel, wastes time, a valuable commodity.

COMMUNICATION STYLE

North Americans tend to be direct and to understand words literally.

A third important dimension of our culture relates to *communication style*. North Americans value straightforwardness, are suspicious of evasiveness, and distrust people who might have a "hidden agenda" or who "play their cards too close to the chest."[14] North Americans also tend to be uncomfortable with silence and impatient with delays. What's more, they tend to use and understand words literally. Latins, on the other hand, enjoy plays on words; Arabs and South Americans sometimes speak with extravagant or poetic figures of speech (such as "the Mother of all battles").

TIME ORIENTATION

North Americans correlate time with productivity, efficiency, and money.

A fourth dimension of our culture relates to *time orientation*. North Americans consider time a precious commodity to be conserved. They correlate time with productivity, efficiency, and money. Keeping people waiting for business appointments wastes time and is also rude. In other cultures, time may be perceived as an unlimited and never-ending resource to be enjoyed. Being late for an appointment is not a grievous sin.

Figure 1.5 compares a number of cultural values for U.S. Americans, Japanese, and Arabs. Notice that belonging, group harmony, and collectiveness are very important to Japanese people, while family matters rank highest with Arabs. As we become aware of the vast differences in cultural values illustrated in Figure 1.5, we can better understand why communication barriers develop and how misunderstandings occur in cross-cultural interactions.

Controlling Ethnocentrism and Stereotyping

The process of understanding and accepting people from other cultures is often hampered by two barriers: ethnocentrism and stereotyping. These two barriers,

FIGURE 1.5

Comparison of Cultural Values Ranked by Priority*

U.S. Americans	Japanese	Arabs
1. Freedom	1. Belonging	1. Family security
2. Independence	2. Group harmony	2. Family harmony
3. Self-reliance	3. Collectiveness	3. Parental guidance
4. Equality	4. Age/Seniority	4. Age
5. Individualism	5. Group consensus	5. Authority
6. Competition	6. Cooperation	6. Compromise
7. Efficiency	7. Quality	7. Devotion
8. Time	8. Patience	8. Patience
9. Directness	9. Indirectness	9. Indirectness
10. Openness	10. Go-between	10. Hospitality

*1 represents the most important value.

Source: Reprinted from *Multicultural Management*, F. Elashmawi and P. R. Harris, p. 72, © 2000 with permission of Elsevier Science.

however, can be overcome by developing tolerance, a powerful and effective aid to communication.

ETHNOCENTRISM

Ethnocentrism is the belief in the superiority of one's own culture and group.

The belief in the superiority of one's own culture is known as *ethnocentrism*. This natural attitude is found in all cultures. Ethnocentrism causes us to judge others by our own values. If you were raised in North America, the values just described probably seem "right" to you, and you may wonder why the rest of the world doesn't function in the same sensible fashion. A North American businessperson in an Arab or Asian country might be upset at time spent over coffee or other social rituals before any "real" business is transacted. In these cultures, however, personal relationships must be established and nurtured before earnest talks may proceed.

STEREOTYPES

A stereotype is an oversimplified behavioral pattern applied to entire groups.

Our perceptions of other cultures sometimes cause us to form stereotypes about groups of people. A *stereotype* is an oversimplified perception of a behavioral pattern or characteristic applied to entire groups. For example, the Swiss are hardworking, efficient, and neat; Germans are formal, reserved, and blunt; Americans are loud, friendly, and impatient; Canadians are polite, trusting, and tolerant; Asians are gracious, humble, and inscrutable. These attitudes may or may not accurately describe cultural norms. When applied to individual business communicators, such stereotypes may create misconceptions and misunderstandings. Look beneath surface stereotypes and labels to discover individual personal qualities.

TOLERANCE

Developing intercultural tolerance means practicing empathy, being nonjudgmental, and being patient.

Working among people from other cultures demands tolerance and flexible attitudes. As global markets expand and as our society becomes increasingly multiethnic, tolerance becomes critical. *Tolerance*, here, does not mean "putting up with" or "enduring," which is one part of its definition. Instead, we use *tolerance* in a broader sense. It means having sympathy for and appreciating beliefs and practices different from our own.

One of the best ways to develop tolerance is by practicing *empathy*. This means trying to see the world through another's eyes. It means being nonjudgmental, recognizing things as they are rather than as they "should be." It includes the ability to accept others' contributions in solving problems in a culturally appropriate manner. When Kal Kan Foods began courting the pet owners of Japan, for example, an Asian advisor suggested that the meat chunks in its Pedigree dog food be cut into perfect little squares. Why? Japanese pet owners feed their dogs piece by piece with chopsticks. Instead of insisting on what "should be" (feeding dogs chunky meat morsels), Kal Kan solved the problem by looking at it from another cultural point of view (providing neat small squares).[15]

The following tips provide specific suggestions for preventing miscommunication in oral and written transactions across cultures.

Tips for Minimizing Oral Miscommunication Among Cross-Cultural Audiences

When you have a conversation with someone from another culture, you can reduce misunderstandings by following these suggestions:

- **Use simple English.** Speak in short sentences (under 20 words) with familiar, short words. Eliminate puns, sports and military references, slang, and jargon (special business terms). Be especially alert to idiomatic expressions that can't be translated, such as *burn the midnight oil* and *under the weather*.
- **Speak slowly and enunciate clearly.** Avoid fast speech, but don't raise your voice. Overpunctuate with pauses and full stops. Always write numbers for all to see.

"He doesn't understand you. Try shouting a little louder."

© 1989 by NEA, Inc.

© BERRY'S WORLD reprinted by permission of Newspaper Enterprise Association, Inc.

- **Encourage accurate feedback.** Ask probing questions, and encourage the listener to paraphrase what you say. Don't assume that a *yes*, a nod, or a smile indicates comprehension or assent.
- **Check frequently for comprehension.** Avoid waiting until you finish a long explanation to request feedback. Instead, make one point at a time, pausing to check for comprehension. Don't proceed to B until A has been grasped.
- **Observe eye messages.** Be alert to a glazed expression or wandering eyes. These tell you the listener is lost.
- **Accept blame.** If a misunderstanding results, graciously accept the blame for not making your meaning clear.
- **Listen without interrupting.** Curb your desire to finish sentences or to fill out ideas for the speaker. Keep in mind that North Americans abroad are often accused of listening too little and talking too much.
- **Remember to smile!** Roger Axtell, international behavior expert, calls the smile the single most understood and most useful form of communication in either personal or business transactions.
- **Follow up in writing.** After conversations or oral negotiations, confirm the results and agreements with follow-up letters. For proposals and contracts, engage a translator to prepare copies in the local language.

Tips for Minimizing Written Miscommunication Among Cross-Cultural Audiences

When you write to someone from a different culture, you can improve your chances of being understood by following these suggestions:

You can improve cross-cultural written communication by adopting local styles, using short sentences and short paragraphs, avoiding ambiguous wording, and citing numbers carefully.

- **Consider local styles.** Learn how documents are formatted and how letters are addressed and developed in the intended reader's country. Decide whether to use your organization's preferred format or adjust to local styles.
- **Consider hiring a translator.** Engage a translator if (1) your document is important, (2) your document will be distributed to many readers, or (3) you must be persuasive.
- **Use short sentences and short paragraphs.** Sentences with fewer than 20 words and paragraphs with fewer than 8 lines are most readable.
- **Avoid ambiguous wording.** Include relative pronouns (*that, which, who*) for clarity in introducing clauses. Stay away from contractions (especially ones like *Here's the problem*). Avoid idioms (*once in a blue moon*), slang (*my presentation really bombed*), acronyms (*ASAP* for *as soon as possible*), abbreviations (*DBA* for *doing business as*), and jargon (*input, output, clickstream*). Use action-specific verbs (*purchase a printer* rather than *get a printer*).
- **Cite numbers carefully.** For international trade it's a good idea to learn and use the metric system. In citing numbers, use figures (*15*) instead of spelling them out (*fifteen*). Always convert dollar figures into local currency. Avoid using figures to express the month of the year. In North America, for example, March 5, 2006, might be written as 3/5/06, while in Europe the same date might appear as 5.3.06. For clarity, always spell out the month.

CAPITALIZING ON WORKFORCE DIVERSITY

As global competition opens world markets, North American businesspeople will increasingly interact with customers and colleagues from around the world. At the same time, the North American workforce is also becoming more diverse—in race, ethnicity, age, gender, national origin, physical ability, and countless other characteristics.

You can expect to be interacting with customers and colleagues who may differ from you in race, ethnicity, age, gender, national origin, physical ability, and many other characteristics.

No longer, say the experts, will the workplace be predominantly male or Anglo-oriented. Nearly 85 percent of the new entrants to the workforce will be women, minorities, and immigrants, according to estimates from the U.S. Bureau of Labor Statistics. By 2012 groups now considered minorities (African Americans, Hispanics, Asians, Native Americans, and others) will make up 34 percent of the workforce. Nearly half (48 percent) of all workers will be women, and more than 19 percent will be fifty-five years or older.[16]

Flatter organizations and emphasis on teamwork increase interactivity within small groups.

While the workforce is becoming more diverse, the structure of many businesses in North America is also changing. As you learned earlier, many workers are now organized by teams. Organizations are flatter, and rank-and-file workers are increasingly making decisions among themselves. What does all this mean for you as a future business communicator? Simply put, your job may require you to interact with colleagues and customers from around the world. Your work environment will probably demand that you cooperate effectively with small groups of coworkers. What's more, these coworkers may differ from you in race, ethnicity, gender, age, and other ways.

A diverse work environment, however, has many benefits. Consumers want to deal with companies that respect their values and create products and services tailored to their needs. Organizations that hire employees with different experiences and backgrounds are better able to create the different products that these consumers desire. In addition, businesses with diverse workforces suffer fewer discrimination lawsuits, fewer union clashes, and less government regulatory action. That's why a growing number of companies view today's diversity movement as a critical bottom-line business strategy. Organizations such as PepsiCo, UPS, Nike, Reebok, and Enterprise Rent-a-Car want employees who speak the same language, literally and figuratively, as their customers.[17] These organizations are convinced that it improves employee relationships and increases business.

Tips for Effective Communication With Diverse Workplace Audiences

Capitalizing on workplace diversity is an enormous challenge for most organizations and individuals. Harmony and acceptance do not follow automatically when people who are dissimilar work together. The following suggestions can help you become a more effective communicator as you enter a rapidly evolving workplace with ethnically diverse colleagues and clients.

Successful communicators understand the value of differences, don't expect conformity, create zero tolerance for bias and stereotypes, and practice open-minded listening.

- **Understand the value of differences.** Diversity makes an organization innovative and creative. Sameness fosters *groupthink*, an absence of critical thinking sometimes found in homogeneous groups. Case studies, for example, of the Kennedy administration's decision to invade Cuba and of the *Challenger*

missile disaster suggest that groupthink prevented alternatives from being considered.[18] Diversity in problem-solving groups encourages independent and creative thinking.

- **Don't expect conformity.** Gone are the days when businesses could say, "This is our culture. Conform or leave." The CEO of athletic shoemaker Reebok stressed seeking people who have new and different stories to tell. "It accomplishes next to nothing to employ those who are different from us if the condition of their employment is that they become the same as us. For it is their differences that enrich us, expand us, provide us the competitive edge."[19]

- **Create zero tolerance for bias and stereotypes.** Cultural patterns exist in every identity group, but applying these patterns to individuals results in stereotyping. Assuming that African Americans are good athletes, that women are poor at math, that French Canadians excel at hockey, or that European American men are insensitive fails to admit the immense differences in people in each group. Check your own use of stereotypes and labels. Don't tell sexist or ethnic jokes at meetings. Avoid slang, abbreviations, and jargon that imply stereotypes. Challenge others' stereotypes politely but firmly.

- **Practice focused, thoughtful, and open-minded listening.** Much misunderstanding can be avoided by attentive listening. Listen for main points; take notes if necessary to remember important details. The most important part of listening, especially among diverse communicators, is judging ideas, not appearances or accents.

Successful communicators invite, use, and give feedback; make few assumptions; learn about their own cultures and other cultures; and seek common ground.

- **Invite, use, and give feedback.** As you learned earlier, a critical element in successful communication is feedback. You can encourage it by asking questions such as *Is there anything you don't understand?* When a listener or receiver responds, use that feedback to adjust your delivery of information. Does the receiver need more details? A different example? Slower delivery? As a good listener, you should also be prepared to give feedback. For example, summarize your understanding of what was said or agreed on.

- **Make fewer assumptions.** Be careful of seemingly insignificant, innocent workplace assumptions. For example, don't assume that everyone wants to observe the holidays with a Christmas party and a decorated tree. Celebrating only Christian holidays in December and January excludes those who honor Hanukkah, Kwanzaa, and the Chinese New Year. Moreover, in workplace discussions don't assume that everyone is married or wants to be or is even heterosexual, for that matter. For invitations, avoid phrases such as "managers and their *wives.*" *Spouses* or *partners* is more inclusive. Valuing diversity means making fewer assumptions that everyone is like you or wants to be like you.

- **Learn about your cultural self.** Knowing your own cultural biases helps you become more objective and adaptable. Begin to recognize the stock reactions and thought patterns that are automatic to you as a result of your upbringing. Become more aware of your own values and beliefs so that you will recognize them when you are confronted by differing values.

Learning about other cultures and seeking common ground help people work together to achieve common goals.

- **Learn about other cultures and identity groups.** People are naturally threatened by the unknown. Consider the following proverb: "I saw in the distance what I took to be a beast, but when I came close, I saw it was my brother and my sister." The same error occurs in communities and work groups. From a distance an unknown person may appear to be threatening. But when the person is recognized or better known, our reactions change. Learning more about diverse groups and individuals helps you reduce the threat of the unknown.

- **Seek common ground.** Look for areas where you and others not like you can agree or share opinions. Be prepared to consider issues from many perspectives, all of which may be valid. Accept that there is room for different points of view to coexist peacefully. Although you can always find differences, it's much harder to find similarities. Look for common ground in shared experiences, mutual goals, and similar values. Concentrate on your objective even when you may disagree on how to reach it.

SUMMING UP AND LOOKING FORWARD

This chapter described the importance of becoming an effective business communicator in this information economy. Many of the changes in today's dynamic workplace revolve around processing and communicating information. Flattened management hierarchies, participatory management, increased emphasis on work teams, heightened global competition, and innovative communication technologies are all trends that increase the need for good communication skills. To improve your skills, you should understand the communication process. Communication doesn't take place unless senders encode meaningful messages that can be decoded and understood by receivers.

One important part of the communication process is listening. You can become a more active listener by keeping an open mind, listening for main points, capitalizing on lag time, judging ideas and not appearances, taking selective notes, and providing feedback. The chapter also described ways to help you improve your nonverbal communication skills.

You learned the powerful effect that culture has on communication, and you became more aware of key cultural values for North Americans. Finally, the chapter discussed ways that businesses and individuals can capitalize on workforce diversity.

The following chapters present the writing process. You will learn specific techniques to help you improve your written and oral expression. Remember, communication skills are not inherited. They are learned. John Bryan, the highly respected former CEO of Sara Lee, recognized this when he said that communication skills are "about 99 percent developed." Bryan contended that "the ability to construct a succinct memo, one that concentrates on the right issues, and the ability to make a presentation to an audience—these are skills that can be taught to almost anyone."[20] Remember that writing skills function as a gatekeeper. Poor skills keep you in low-wage, dead-end work. Good skills open the door to high wages and career advancement.[21]

CRITICAL THINKING

1. Why is it important for business and professional students to develop good communication skills, and why is it difficult or impossible to do without help?

2. Recall a time when you experienced a problem as a result of poor communication. What were the causes of and possible remedies for the problem?

3. How are listening skills important to employees, supervisors, and executives? Who should have the best listening skills?

4. What arguments could you give for or against the idea that body language is a science with principles that can be interpreted accurately by specialists?

5. Because English is becoming the world's language and because the United States is a dominant military and trading force, why should Americans bother to learn about other cultures?

CHAPTER REVIEW

6. Are communication skills acquired by *nature* or by *nurture*? Explain.

7. List seven trends in the workplace that affect business communicators. Be prepared to discuss how they might affect you in your future career.

8. Give a brief definition of the following words:
   a. Encode
   b. Channel
   c. Decode

9. List 11 techniques for improving your listening skills. Be prepared to discuss each.

10. What is nonverbal communication? Give several examples.

11. Name five unprofessional communication techniques that can sabotage a career.

12. Describe the concept of North American individualism. How does this concept set North Americans apart from people in some other cultures?

13. What is ethnocentrism, and how can it be reduced?

14. List seven suggestions for enhancing comprehension when you are talking with people for whom English is a second language. Be prepared to discuss each.

15. List at least eight suggestions for becoming a more effective communicator in a diverse workplace. Be prepared to discuss each.

EXPAND YOUR LEARNING WITH THESE BONUS RESOURCES!

Guffey Companion Web Site

http://guffey.swlearning.com

Your companion Web site offers review quizzes, a glossary of key terms, and flash cards to build your knowledge of chapter concepts. Additional career tools include *Dr. Guffey's Guide to Business Etiquette and Workplace Manners*, *Listening Quiz*, and electronic citation formats (MLA and APA) for business writers. You'll also find updated links to all chapter URLs.

Guffey Xtra!

http://guffeyxtra.swlearning.com

This online study assistant illustrates chapter concepts in PowerPoint. It strengthens your language skills with *Your Personal Language Trainer* (a grammar/mechanics review), *Speak Right!*, *Spell Right!*, and *Sentence Competency Exercises*. In addition, **Guffey Xtra!** brings you bonus online chapters: *Employment and Other Interviewing* and *How to Write Instructions*. You'll also find the Grammar/Mechanics Challenge exercises so that you can revise without rekeying.

INFOTRAC COLLEGE EDITION

Building Knowledge and Research Skills

To excel as a knowledge worker in today's digital workplace, you must know how to find and evaluate information on the Internet. As a student purchasing a new copy of Guffey's *Essentials of Business Communication*, 7e, you have an extraordinary opportunity to develop these research skills. For four months you have special access to InfoTrac College Edition, a comprehensive Web-based collection of millions of journal, magazine, encyclopedia, and newspaper articles. You'll find many activities and study questions in this text that help you build knowledge and develop research skills using InfoTrac. Watch for the InfoTrac icons. InfoTrac is available only with NEW copies of your textbook.

How to Use InfoTrac

With your Web browser on your computer screen, key the following URL: www.infotrac-college.com. Click *Register New Account*. Establish your logon name and password. (You may wish to read Thomson's Privacy Policy). When you feel confident, go to the *Keyword Search* page and enter your search term. If you need a little help, click *InfoTrac Demo*.

ACTIVITIES AND CASES

1.1 Pumping Up Your Basic Language Muscles With Xtra!

You can enlist the aid of your author to help you pump up your basic language skills. As your personal trainer, Dr. Guffey provides a three-step workout plan and hundreds of interactive questions to help you brush up on your grammar and mechanics skills. You receive immediate feedback in the warm-up sessions, and when you finish a complete workout you can take a short test to assess what you learned. These workouts are completely self-teaching, which means you can review at your own pace and repeat as often as you need. *Your Personal Language Trainer* is available to you at http://guffeyxtra.swlearning.com. In addition to pumping up your basic language muscles, you can also use *Spell Right!* and *Speak Right!* to improve your spelling and pronunciation skills.

Your Task. Begin using *Your Personal Language Trainer* to brush up your basic grammar and mechanics skills by completing one to three workouts per week or as many as your instructor advises. Be prepared to submit a printout of your "fitness" (completion) certificate when you finish a workout module. If your instructor directs, complete the spelling exercises in *Spell Right!* and submit a certificate of completion for the spelling final exam.

1.2 Getting To Know You

Because today's work and class environments often involve cooperating in teams or small groups, getting to know your fellow classmates is important. To learn something about the people in this class and to give you practice in developing your communication skills, your instructor may choose one of the following activities:

Your Task

a.   For larger classes, divide into groups of four or five. Take one minute to introduce yourself briefly (name, major interest, hobbies, goals) within your group. Spend five minutes in the first group session. Record the first name of each individual you meet. Then informally regroup. In new groups again spend five minutes on introductions. After three or four sessions, study your name list. How many names can you associate with faces?

b.   For smaller classes, introduce yourself in a two-minute oral presentation while standing before the class at the rostrum. Where are you from? What are your educational goals? What are your interests? What do you expect from this class? This informal presentation may serve as the first of two or three oral presentations correlated with Chapter 12.

c.   For online classes, write a letter of introduction about yourself answering the questions in (b). Post your letter to your discussion board. Read and comment on the letters of other students. Think about how people in virtual teams must learn about each other through online messages.

1.3 Class Listening

Have you ever consciously observed the listening habits of others?

Your Task. In one of your classes, study student listening habits for a week. What barriers to effective listening did you observe? How many of the suggestions described in this chapter are being implemented by listeners in the class? Write a memo or an e-mail message to your instructor briefly describing your observations. (See Chapter 5 to learn more about memos.)

1.4 How Good Are Your Listening Skills? Self-Checked Rating Quiz

You can learn whether your listening skills are excellent or deficient by completing a brief quiz.

Your Task. Take Dr. Guffey's Listening Quiz at *http://guffey.swlearning.com*. What two listening behaviors do you think you need to work on the most?

INFOTRAC

1.5 Finding Relevant Listening Advice

Your manager, Rasheed Love, has been asked to be part of a panel discussion at a management conference. The topic is "Workplace Communication Challenges," and his area of expertise is listening. He asks you to help him prepare for the discussion by doing some research.

Your Task. Using an InfoTrac subject search, locate at least three articles with suggestions for improving workplace listening skills. Use full-text articles, not abstracts. In a memo to Rasheed Love, present a two- to three-sentence summary explaining why each article is helpful. Include the author's name, publication, date of publication, and page number. Then list at least ten listening suggestions. See Chapter 5 for memo format. Begin your memo with a sentence such as, "As you requested, I found three articles on listening techniques. After discussing the articles, I will present a list with the most helpful suggestions."

1.6 Silent Messages

Becoming more aware of the silent messages you send helps you make them more accurate.

Your Task. Analyze the kinds of silent messages you send your instructor, your classmates, and your employer. How do you send these messages? Group them into categories, as suggested by what you learned in this chapter. What do these messages mean? Be prepared to discuss them in small groups or in a memo to your instructor.

1.7 Body Language

Can body language be accurately interpreted?

Your Task. What attitudes do the following body movements suggest to you? Do these movements always mean the same thing? What part does context play in your interpretations?

a. Whistling, wringing hands

b. Bowed posture, twiddling thumbs

c. Steepled hands, sprawling sitting position

d. Rubbing hand through hair

e. Open hands, unbuttoned coat

f. Wringing hands, tugging ears

1.8 Universal Sign For "I Goofed"

In an effort to promote peace and tranquillity on the highways, motorists submitted the following suggestions to a newspaper columnist.[22]

Your Task. In small groups consider the pros and cons for each of the following gestures intended as an apology when a driver makes a mistake. Why would some fail?

a. Lower your head slightly and bonk yourself on the forehead with the side of your closed fist. The message is clear: "I'm stupid. I shouldn't have done that."

b. Make a temple with your hands, as if you were praying.

c. Move the index finger of your right hand back and forth across your neck—as if you were cutting your throat.

d. Flash the well-known peace sign. Hold up the index and middle fingers of one hand, making a *V*, as in Victory.

e. Place the flat of your hands against your cheeks, as children do when they've made a mistake.

f. Clasp your hand over your mouth, raise your brows, and shrug your shoulders.

g. Use your knuckles to knock on the side of your head. Translation: "Oops! Engage brain."

h. Place your right hand high on your chest and pat a few times, like a basketball player who drops a pass or a football player who makes a bad throw. This says, "I'll take the blame."

i. Place your right fist over the middle of your chest and move it in a circular motion. This is universal sign language for "I'm sorry."

j. Open your window and tap the top of your car roof with your hand.

k. Smile and raise both arms, palms outward, which is a universal gesture for surrender or forgiveness.

l. Use the military salute, which is simple and shows respect.

m. Flash your biggest smile, point at yourself with your right thumb and move your head from left to right, as if to say, "I can't believe I did that."

1.9 Alice In Wonderland Travels to Tokyo

Jeff Davis is the leader of a creative team representing a large American theme park company. The owners of a Japanese park rely on the American company to develop new attractions for their Tokyo park. But the Japanese own their park and must approve any new addition. Jeff and his team recently traveled to Japan to make an important presentation to the owners. His team had worked for the past year developing the concept of an outdoor garden maze with a network of hedge passageways for children to wander through. The concept was based on *Alice in Wonderland*.

The jobs of Jeff's entire team depended on selling the idea of this new attraction (including restaurants and gift shops) to the owners of the Tokyo park. Because the Japanese smiled and nodded throughout the presentation, Jeff assumed they liked the idea. When he pushed for final approval, the Japanese smiled and said that an outdoor garden attraction might be difficult in their climate. Jeff explained away that argument. Then, he asked for a straightforward *yes* or *no*, but the Japanese answered, "We will have to study it very carefully." Thinking he had not made himself clear, Jeff began to review the strong points of the presentation.

Your Task. Analyze the preceding cross-cultural incident. What cultural elements may be interfering with communication in this exchange?

TEAM   **CRITICAL THINKING**

1.10 Cross-Cultural Gap At Resort Hotel In Thailand

The Laguna Beach Resort Hotel in Phuket, Thailand, nestled between a tropical lagoon and the sparkling Andaman Sea, is one of the most beautiful resorts in the world. Fortunately, it was spared serious damage from the region's tidal waves. (You can take a virtual tour by using Google and searching for "Laguna Beach Resort Phuket.") When Brett Peel arrived as the director of the hotel's kitchen, he thought he had landed in paradise. Only on the job six weeks, he began wondering why his Thai staff would answer *yes* even when they didn't understand what he had said. Other foreign managers discovered that junior staff managers rarely spoke up and never expressed an opinion contrary to those of senior executives. What's more, guests with a complaint thought that Thai employees were not taking them seriously because the Thais smiled at even the worst complaints. Thais also did not seem to understand deadlines or urgent requests.[23]

Your Task. In teams decide how you would respond to the following. If you were the director of this hotel, would you implement a training program for employees? If so, would you train only foreign managers, or would you include local Thai employees as well? What topics should a training program include? Would your goal be to introduce Western ways to the Thais? At least 90 percent of the hotel guests are non-Thai.

1.11 Translating Idioms

Many languages have idiomatic expressions that do not always make sense to outsiders.

Your Task. Explain in simple English what the following idiomatic expressions mean. Assume that you are explaining them to people for whom English is a second language.

a.   class act

b.   grey area

c.   cold shoulder

d.   eager beaver

e.   early bird

f.   get your act together

g.   go ape

h.   go behind someone's back

i.   the bottom of the barrel

1.12 Analyzing Diversity At Reebok

Reebok grew from a $12 million a year sport shoe company into a $3 billion footwear and apparel powerhouse without giving much thought to the hiring of employees. "When we were growing very, very fast, all we did was bring another friend into work the next day," recalled Sharon Cohen, Reebok vice president. "Everybody hired nine of their friends. Well, it happened that nine white people hired nine of their friends, so guess what? They were white, all about the same age. And then we looked up and said, 'Wait a minute. We don't like the way it looks here.' That's the kind of thing that can happen when you are growing very fast and thoughtlessly."[24]

Your Task. In what ways would Reebok benefit by diversifying its staff? What competitive advantages might it gain? Outline your reasoning in an e-mail message to your instructor.

VIDEO RESOURCES

Two special sets of videos accompany Guffey's *Essentials of Business Communication*, 7e. These videos take you beyond the classroom to build the communication skills you will need to succeed in today's rapidly changing workplace.

Video Library 1, *Building Workplace Communication Skills*, presents five videos that introduce and reinforce concepts in selected chapters. These excellent tools ease the learning load by demonstrating chapter-specific material to strengthen your comprehension and retention of key ideas.

Video Library 2, *Bridging the Gap*, presents six videos transporting you inside high-profile companies such as Yahoo, Ben & Jerry's, and Zubi Advertising. You'll be able to apply your new skills in structured applications aimed at bridging the gap between the classroom and the real world of work.

We recommend two videos for this chapter:

Career Success Starts With Communication Foundations. This film, made especially for Guffey books, illustrates the changing business world, flattened management hierarchies, the communication process, communication flow, ethics, listening, nonverbal communication, and other topics to prepare you for today's workplace. The film is unique in that many concepts are demonstrated through role-playing. Be prepared to discuss critical-thinking questions at the film's conclusion.

Erasing Stereotypes: Zubi Advertising. This film features a successful businessperson who used her knowledge of Hispanic culture to build an advertising company that creates ads appealing to the Hispanic American market. Despite the obstacles of being a female and a Cuban in Miami, Teresa Zubizarreta created a hugely successful advertising agency. With headquarters in Miami and satellite offices in Los Angeles, Chicago, Houston, Detroit, and New York, Teresa Zubizarreta and her 70-person team work to craft precise messages aimed at Hispanic audiences. Your instructor may ask you to watch for specific information as you view this film.

● GRAMMAR/MECHANICS CHECKUP—1

These checkups are designed to improve your control of grammar and mechanics. They systematically review all sections of the Grammar/Mechanics Handbook. Answers are provided near the end of the book. You will find Advanced Grammar/Mechanics Checkups with immediate feedback at **Guffey Xtra!** (*http://guffeyxtra.swlearning.com*).

Nouns

Review Sections 1.02–1.06 in the Grammar/Mechanics Handbook. Then study each of the following statements. Underscore any inappropriate form, and write a correction in the space provided. Also record the appropriate G/M section and letter to illustrate the principle involved. If a sentence is correct, write *C*. When you finish, compare your responses with those provided. If your answers differ, study carefully the principles shown in parentheses.

<u>attorneys</u>   (1.05d)   **Example**   <u>Attornies</u> seem to be the only ones who benefit from class action suits.

1. Some companys are giving up land lines and using cell phones exclusively.
2. Business is better on Saturday's than on Sundays.
3. Some of the citys in Craig's report offer excellent opportunities.
4. Frozen chickens and turkies are kept in the company's lockers.
5. All secretaries were asked to check supplies and other inventorys.
6. Only the Bushs and the Sanchezes brought their entire families.
7. In the 1990s profits grew rapidly; in the late 2000's investments soared.
8. Both editor in chiefs instituted strict proofreading policies.
9. Luxury residential complexs are part of the architect's plan.
10. Voters in three countys are likely to approve new gas taxes.
11. The instructor was surprised to find two Cassidy's in one class.
12. André sent digital photos of two valleys in France before we planned our trip.
13. Most companies have copies of statements showing their assets and liabilitys.
14. My flat-screen monitor makes it difficult to distinguish between o's and a's.
15. Both runner-ups complained about the winner's behavior.

GRAMMAR/MECHANICS CHALLENGE—1

The following memo has many faults in grammar, spelling, punctuation, capitalization, word use, and number form. Correct the errors with standard proofreading marks (see Appendix B) or revise the message online at **Guffey Xtra!** Study the guidelines in the Grammar/Mechanics Handbook to sharpen your skills. When you finish, your instructor can show you the revised version of this memo.

TO: Jocelyn Smith-Garcia

FROM: Kevin West, Manager

DATE: November 4, 200x

SUBJECT: SUGGESTION FOR TELECOMMUTING SUCCESSFULLY

To help you become an effective telecommuter Jocelyn, we have a few suggestions to share with you. I understand you will be working at home for the next 9 months. The following guidelines should help you stay in touch with us, and compleate your work satisfactory.

- Be sure to check your message bored daily, and respond immediate to those who are trying to reach you.

- Check your e-mail at least 3 times a day, answer all messages promply, make sure that you sent copys of relevent message's to the appropriate officestaff.

- Transmit all spread sheet work to Zachary Jacksen in our computer services department, he will analyze each week's activitys, and update all inventorys.

- Provide me with end of week reports' indicating the major accounts you serviced.

In prepareing your work area you should make sure you have adequate space for your computer printer fax and storage. For Security reasons you're workingarea should be off limits to your family and friends.

We will continue to hold once a week staff meetings on Friday's at 10 a.m. in the morning. Do you think it would be possible for you to attend 1 or 2 of these meeting. The next one is Friday November 17th.

I know you will enjoy working at home Joclyn. Following these basic guidelines should help you accomplish your work, and provide the office with adequate contact with you.

Communication Workshops (such as the one on the next page) provide insight into special business communication topics and skills not discussed in the chapters. These topics cover ethics, technology, career skills, and collaboration. Each workshop includes a career application with a case study or problem to help you develop skills relevant to the workshop topic.

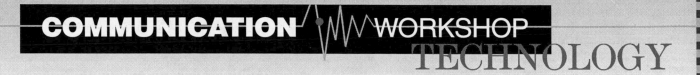

USING JOB BOARDS TO LEARN ABOUT
EMPLOYMENT POSSIBILITIES IN YOUR FIELD

Nearly everyone looking for a job today starts with the Web. This communication workshop will help you use the Web to study job openings in your field. Locating jobs or internships on the Web has distinct advantages. For a few job seekers, the Web leads to bigger salaries, wider opportunities, and faster hiring. The Web, however, can devour huge chunks of time and produce slim results.

In terms of actually finding a job, using the Web does not always result in success. Web searching seems to work best for professionals looking for similar work in their current fields and for those who are totally flexible about location. Yet, the Web is an excellent place for any job seeker to learn what's available, what qualifications are necessary, and what salaries are being offered. Thousands of job boards with many job listings for employers across the United States and abroad are available on the Web.

Career Application. Assume that you are about to finish your degree or certification program, and you are now looking for a job. At the direction of your instructor, conduct a survey of electronic job advertisements in your field. What's available? How much is the salary? What are the requirements?

Your Task

- **Visit Monster.com** *<www.monster.com>*, one of the most popular job boards.

- **Study the opening page.** Remember that most job boards are supported by advertisements. As a result, you might get a pop-up ad, which you should ignore. Close any pop-up boxes. From the opening page, click *Find Jobs*.

- **Read *More Search Tips*.** Before entering any keywords, it's wise to spend a few moments learning how to search. Click *More Search Tips* for many helpful hints on precise searching. Browsing this information may take a few minutes, but it's well worth the effort. Scroll down to learn about safe job searching, keyword searching, location and company searching, and sorting and viewing your results. Close this box by clicking the *X* in the top right corner.

- **Conduct a practice search.** Back on the search page, enter a search term in the *Enter Key Word(s)* box. Skip the *Enter Company Name* box and then click a geographical area in the *Select Location* box. Just for fun, try "Honolulu, Hawaii." In the *Select Job Category* box, select an appropriate term, such as Advertising or Accounting. Then press click *Get Results*. You should see many current job ads.

- **Conduct a real search.** Now conduct a job search in your career area and in geographical areas of your choice. Select three ads and print them. If you cannot print, make notes on what you find.

- **Visit another site.** Try *www.CollegeRecruiter.com*, which claims to be the highest-traffic entry-level job site for students and graduates, or *www.careerbuilder.com*, which says it is the nation's largest employment network. Become familiar with the site's searching tools, and look for jobs in your field. Select and print three ads.

- **Analyze the skills required.** From the ads you printed, how often do they mention communication, teamwork, computer skills, or professionalism? What tasks do the ads mention? What is the salary range identified in these ads for this position? Your instructor may ask you to submit your findings and/or report to the class.

CHAPTER 5

E-MAIL AND MEMORANDUMS

> *E-mail is changing our behavior, our way of interacting with people, our institutions. And it is happening incredibly fast. . . . Because it's spread so fast, it has raced ahead of our abilities to fully adapt to this new form of communication.*
>
> **Michael D. Eisner**, former CEO, Walt Disney Company[1]

OBJECTIVES

- Analyze the writing process and how it helps you produce effective e-mail messages and memos.

- Discuss the structure and formatting of e-mail messages and memos.

- Describe smart e-mail practices, including getting started; content, tone, and correctness; netiquette; reading and replying to e-mail; personal use; and other practices.

- Write information and procedure e-mail messages and memos.

- Write request and reply e-mail messages and memos.

APPLYING THE WRITING PROCESS TO PRODUCE EFFECTIVE E-MAIL MESSAGES AND MEMOS

As former Disney CEO Michael Eisner recognized, e-mail has transformed many aspects of our lives, especially the way business is conducted. Written communication to anyone within the office or almost anywhere in the world can now be completed nearly instantaneously. In the past, internal communication (written messages within organizations) generally took the form of hard-copy memorandums. In today's workplace e-mail is increasingly the communication channel of choice for most internal and many external messages. Business leaders such as Michael Eisner recognize the functions and benefits but also the potential dangers of e-mail.

E-mail is increasingly the channel of choice for internal messages and even for many external messages.

A primary function of e-mail is exchanging messages within organizations. Such internal communication has taken on increasing importance today. Organizations are downsizing, flattening chains of command, forming work teams, and empowering rank-and-file employees. Given more power in making decisions, employees find that they need more information. They must collect, exchange, and evaluate information about the products and services they offer. Management also needs input from

Former Disney CEO Michael Eisner thinks long and hard before dashing off e-mail messages, especially when he's angry. "I learned early in the hard paper world of the '70s that when I was annoyed with someone, I should write it down in a memo. I would then put the memo in my desk drawer and leave it there until the next day." By the next morning, his anger had passed; and he realized that telephoning or seeing the other person was a better way to respond.

© SCOTT AUDETTE/AP WIDE WORLD PHOTOS

employees to respond rapidly to local and global market changes. This growing demand for information means an increasing use of e-mail, although hard-copy memos are still written.

Skillful documents get the job done and make you look professional.

Developing skill in writing e-mail messages and memos brings you two important benefits. First, well-written documents are likely to achieve their goals. They create goodwill by being cautious, caring, and clear. They do not intentionally or unintentionally create ill feelings. Second, well-written internal messages enhance your image within the organization. Individuals identified as competent, professional writers are noticed and rewarded; most often, they are the ones promoted into management positions.

This chapter concentrates on direct e-mail messages and memos. These straightforward messages open with the main idea because their topics are not sensitive and require little persuasion. You'll study the writing process as well as the structure and format of e-mail messages and memos. Because e-mail is such a powerful channel of communication, we'll devote special attention to composing smart e-mail messages and reading and responding to e-mail professionally. Finally, you'll learn to write procedure, information, request, and reply messages.

Careful writing takes time—especially at first. By following a systematic plan and practicing your skill, however, you can speed up your efforts and greatly improve the product. Let's review the three-phase writing process to see how it applies to e-mail messages and memos.

Phase 1: Analysis, Anticipation, and Adaptation

Before writing, ask questions that help you analyze, anticipate, and adapt your message.

In Phase 1, prewriting, you'll need to spend some time analyzing your task. It's amazing how many of us are ready to put our pens or computers into gear before engaging our minds. Before writing, ask yourself these important questions:

- **Do I really need to write this e-mail or memo?** A phone call or a quick visit to a nearby coworker might solve the problem—and save the time and expense of a written message. On the other hand, some written messages are needed to provide a permanent record.
- **Should I send an e-mail or a hard-copy memo?** It's tempting to use e-mail for all your correspondence. But a phone call or face-to-face visit is a better channel choice if you need to (1) convey enthusiasm, warmth, or other emotion; (2) supply a context; or (3) smooth over disagreements.

Randy Glasbergen.
www.glasbergen.com

"Be careful what you write. My wonderful, charming, brilliant boss reads everyone's e-mail."

- **Why am I writing?** Know why you are writing and what you hope to achieve. This will help you recognize what the important points are and where to place them.
- **How will the reader react?** Visualize the reader and the effect your message will have. In writing e-mail messages and memos, imagine that you are sitting and talking with your reader. Avoid speaking bluntly, failing to explain, or ignoring your reader's needs. Consider ways to shape the message to benefit the reader. Also be careful about what you say because your message may very well be forwarded to someone else—or may be read by your boss.
- **How can I save my reader's time?** Think of ways that you can make your message easier to comprehend at a glance. Use bullets, asterisks, lists, headings, and white space to improve readability.

Phase 2: Research, Organization, and Composition

Gather background information; organize it into an outline; compose your message; and revise for clarity, correctness, and feedback.

Phase 2, writing, involves gathering documentation, organizing, and actually composing the first draft. Although some of your e-mail messages and memos will be short, you'll want to follow these steps in the process to ensure an effective message:

- **Conduct research.** Check the files, talk with your boss, and possibly consult the target audience to collect information before you begin to write. Gather any documentation necessary to support your message.
- **Organize your information.** Make a brief outline of the points you want to cover in your message. For short messages jot down notes on the document you are answering or make a scratch list at your computer.
- **Compose your first draft.** At your computer compose the message from your outline. As you compose, avoid amassing huge blocks of text. No one wants to read endless lines of type. Instead, group related information into paragraphs, preferably short ones. Paragraphs separated by white space look inviting. Be sure each paragraph begins with the main point and is backed up by details. If you bury your main point in the middle of a paragraph, it may be missed.

Phase 3: Revision, Proofreading, and Evaluation

Phase 3, revising, involves putting the final touches on your message. Careful and caring writers will ask a number of questions as they do the following:

- **Revise for clarity and conciseness.** Viewed from the receiver's perspective, are the ideas clear? Do they need more explanation? If the message is passed on to others, will they need further explanation? Consider having a colleague critique your message if it is an important one.
- **Proofread for correctness.** Are the sentences complete and punctuated properly? Did you overlook any typos or misspelled words? Remember to use your spell checker and grammar checker to proofread your message before sending it.
- **Plan for feedback.** How will you know whether this message is successful? You can improve feedback by asking questions (such as *Are you comfortable with these suggestions?* or *What do you think?*). Remember to make it easy for the receiver to respond.

ANALYZING THE STRUCTURE AND FORMAT OF E-MAIL MESSAGES AND MEMOS

E-mail messages and memos inform employees, request data, give responses, confirm decisions, and provide directions.

Whether electronic or hard copy, direct e-mail messages and memos generally contain four parts: (1) an informative subject line that summarizes the message, (2) an opening that reveals the main idea immediately, (3) a body that explains and justifies the main idea, and (4) an appropriate closing.

Writing the Subject Line

Subject lines summarize the purpose of the message in abbreviated form.

In e-mails and memos an informative subject line is mandatory. It summarizes the central idea, thus providing quick identification for reading and for filing. In e-mail messages, subject lines are essential. Busy readers glance at a subject line and decide whether and when to read the message. Those without subject lines are often automatically deleted.

What does it take to get your message read? For one thing, stay away from meaningless or dangerous words. A sure way to get your message deleted or ignored is to use a one-word heading such as *Issue, Problem, Important*, or *Help*. Including a word such as *Free* is dangerous because it may trigger spam filters. Try to make your subject line "talk" by including a verb. Explain the purpose of the message and how it relates to the reader (*Need You to Showcase Two Items at Our Next Trade Show* rather than *Trade Show*). Finally, update your subject line to reflect the current message (*Staff Meeting Rescheduled for May 12* rather than *Re: Re: Staff Meeting*). A subject line is usually written in an abbreviated style, often without articles (*a, an, the*). It need not be a complete sentence, and it does not end with a period.

Opening With the Main Idea

Direct e-mails and memos open by revealing the main idea immediately.

Most e-mails and memos cover nonsensitive information that can be handled in a straightforward manner. Begin by frontloading; that is, reveal the main idea immediately. Even though the purpose of the memo or e-mail is summarized in the subject line, that purpose should be restated—and amplified—in the first sentence. Busy readers want to know immediately why they are reading a message. As you learned in Chapter 3, most messages should begin directly. Notice how the following indirect opener can be improved by frontloading.

Indirect Opening	Direct Opening
For the past six months the Human Resources Development Department has been considering changes in our employee benefit plan.	Please review the following proposal regarding employee benefits, and let me know by May 20 if you approve these changes.

Explaining in the Body

Designed for easy comprehension, the body explains one topic.

The body provides more information about the reason for writing. It explains and discusses the subject logically. Good e-mail messages and memos generally discuss only one topic. Limiting the topic helps the receiver act on the subject and file it appropriately. A writer who, for example, describes a computer printer problem and also requests permission to attend a conference runs a 50 percent failure risk. The reader may respond to the printer problem but forget about the conference request.

The body of e-mail messages and memos should have high *skim value*. This means that information should be easy to read and comprehend. Three techniques for improving readability include lists, headings, and graphics techniques.

Because business communicators often juggle many tasks and projects at the same time, they appreciate e-mail messages that are well-organized with listed items and headings that provide high "skim value."

© ROYALTY-FREE/COMSTOCK/GETTY IMAGES

USING NUMBERED AND BULLETED LISTS FOR QUICK COMPREHENSION

One of the best ways to ensure rapid comprehension of ideas is through the use of numbered or bulleted lists. Ideas formerly buried within sentences or paragraphs stand out when listed. Readers not only understand your message more rapidly and easily but also consider you efficient and well organized. Lists provide high "skim value." This means that readers use lists to read quickly and grasp main ideas. By breaking up complex information into smaller chunks, lists improve readability, comprehension, and retention. They also force the writer to organize ideas and write efficiently. Use numbered lists for items that represent a sequence or reflect a numbering system. Use bulleted lists to highlight items that don't necessarily show a chronology.

Numbered lists represent sequences; bulleted lists highlight items that may not show a sequence.

Numbered List	Bulleted List
Our recruiters follow these steps in hiring applicants:	To attract upscale customers, we feature the following:
1. Examine the application.	• Quality fashions
2. Interview the applicant.	• Personalized service
3. Check the applicant's references.	• A generous return policy

In listing items vertically, capitalize the word at the beginning of each line. Add end punctuation only if the statements are complete sentences. Be sure to use parallel construction. Notice in the numbered list that each item begins with a verb. In the bulleted list each item follows an adjective/noun sequence. Be careful, however, not to overuse the list format. One writing expert warns that too many lists make messages look like grocery lists.[2]

ADDING HEADINGS FOR VISUAL IMPACT

Headings that summarize ideas enable readers to preview and review quickly.

Headings are another important tool for highlighting information and improving readability. They encourage the writer to organize carefully so that similar material is grouped together. This helps the reader separate major ideas from details. Moreover, headings enable a busy reader to skim familiar or less important information. They also provide a quick preview or review. Headings appear most often in reports, which you'll study in greater detail in Unit 4. However, main headings, subheadings,

Effective category headings summarize topics in parallel form to help readers grasp ideas quickly.

and category headings can also improve readability in e-mail messages, memos, and letters. Here, they are used with bullets to summarize categories:

Category Headings

Our company focuses on the following areas in the employment process:

- **Attracting applicants.** We advertise for qualified applicants, and we also encourage current employees to recommend good people.
- **Interviewing applicants.** Our specialized interviews include simulated customer encounters as well as scrutiny by supervisors.
- **Checking references.** We investigate every applicant thoroughly, including conversations with former employers and all listed references.

IMPROVING READABILITY WITH OTHER GRAPHICS TECHNIQUES

Vertical lists and headings are favorite tools for improving readability, but other graphics techniques can also focus attention.

To highlight individual words, use CAPITAL letters, underlining, **bold** type, or *italics*. Be careful with these techniques, though, because readers may feel they are being shouted at.

One final technique to enhance comprehension is blank space. Space is especially important in e-mail messages when formatting techniques don't always work. Grouping ideas under capitalized headings with blank space preceding the heading can greatly improve readability.

Closing With a Purpose

Messages should close with (1) action information including dates and deadlines, (2) a summary, or (3) a closing thought.

Generally close an e-mail message or a memo with (1) action information, dates, or deadlines; (2) a summary of the message; or (3) a closing thought. Here again the value of thinking through the message before actually writing it becomes apparent. The closing is where readers look for deadlines and action language. An effective memo or e-mail closing might be, *Please submit your report by June 15 so that we can have your data before our July planning session.*

In more complex messages a summary of main points may be an appropriate closing. If no action request is made and a closing summary is unnecessary, you might end with a simple concluding thought (*I'm glad to answer your questions* or *This sounds like a useful project*). You needn't close messages to coworkers with goodwill statements such as those found in letters to customers or clients. However, some closing thought is often necessary to prevent a feeling of abruptness. Closings can show gratitude or encourage feedback with remarks such as *I sincerely appreciate your help* or *What are your ideas on this proposal?* Other closings look forward to what's next, such as *How would you like to proceed?* Avoid closing with overused expressions such as *Please let me know if I may be of further assistance.* This ending sounds mechanical and insincere.

Putting It All Together

Now let's follow the development of a routine information e-mail message to see how we can apply the ideas just discussed. Figure 5.1 shows the first draft of an e-mail message James Perkins, marketing manager, wrote to his boss, Jie Wang. Although it contained solid information, the message was so wordy and dense that the main points were submerged.

After writing the first draft, James realized that he needed to reorganize his message into an opening, body, and closing. He also desperately needed to improve the readability. In studying what he had written, he realized that he was talking about two main problems. He also discovered that he could present a three-part solution. These ideas didn't occur to him until he had written the first draft. Only in the revision stage was he able to see in his own mind that he was talking about two separate problems

FIGURE 5.1   • **Information E-Mail Message**

before revision

To   Jie Wang <jwang@edison.com>
From   James Perkins <jperkins@edison.com>
Subject: Problems •

This is in response to your recent inquiry about our customer database. Your message of •
May 9 said that you wanted to know how to deal with the database problems.

I can tell you that the biggest problem is that it contains a lot of outdated information,
including customers who haven't purchased anything in five or more years. Another •
problem is that the old database is not compatible with the new Access software that is
being used by our mailing service, and this makes it difficult to merge files.

I think I can solve both problems, however, by starting a new database. This would be
the place where we put the names of all new customers. And we would have it
keyed using Access software. The problem with outdated information could be solved by •
finding out if the customers in our old database wish to continue receiving our newsletter
and product announcements. Finally, we would rekey the names of all active customers
in the new database.

Uses meaningless
subject line

Fails to reveal
purpose quickly

Buries two problems and three-part
solution in huge paragraph

Forgets to conclude with
next action and end date

after revision

Informative subject line
summarizes purpose

Opening states
purpose concisely
and highlights
two problems

Body organizes
main points
for readability

Closing includes
key benefit, deadline,
and next action

File Edit Mailbox Message Transfer Special Tools Window Help

B / U   Send

To: Jie Wang <jwang@edison.com>
From: James Perkins <jperkins@edison.com>
• **Subject:** Recommendations for Improving Our Customer Database

Jie:

As you requested, I am submitting my recommendations for improving our customer database.
The database has two major problems. First, it contains many names of individuals who have
not made purchases in five or more years. Second, the format is not compatible with the new
Access software used by our mailing service.

The following three steps, however, should solve both problems:

1. START A NEW DATABASE. Effective immediately enter the names of all new customers in a
new database using Access software.

2. DETERMINE THE STATUS OF CUSTOMERS in our old database. Send out a mailing asking
whether recipients wish to continue receiving our newsletter and product announcements.

3. REKEY THE NAMES OF ACTIVE CUSTOMERS. Enter the names of all responding customers
in our new database so that we have only one active database.

These changes will enable you, as team leader, to request mailings that go only to active
customers. Please let me know by May 20 whether you think these recommendations are
workable. If so, I will investigate costs.

James

as well as a three-part solution. The revision process can help you think through a problem and clarify a solution.

In the revised version, James was more aware of the subject line, opening, body, and closing. He used an informative subject line and opened directly by explaining why he was writing. His opening also outlined the two main problems so that his reader understood the background of the following recommendations. In the body of his message, James identified three corrective actions, and he highlighted them for improved readability. Notice that he listed his three recommendations using numbers (bullets don't always transmit well in e-mail messages) with capitalized headings. Numbers, asterisks, white space, and capitalized letters work well in e-mail messages to highlight important points. Notice, too, that James closed his message with a deadline and a reference to the next action to be taken.

Formatting E-Mail Messages

Because e-mail is a developing communication channel, its formatting and usage conventions are still fluid. Users and authorities, for instance, do not always agree on what's appropriate for salutations and closings. The following suggestions, however, can guide you in formatting most e-mail messages, but always check with your organization to observe its practices.

GUIDE WORDS

Following the guide word *To*, some writers insert just the recipient's electronic address, such as *mphilly@accountpro.com*. Other writers prefer to include the receiver's full name plus the electronic address, as shown in Figure 5.2. By including full names in the *To* and *From* slots, both receivers and senders are better able to identify the message. By the way, the order of *Date, To, From, Subject*, and other guide words varies depending on your e-mail program and whether you are sending or receiving the message.

Most e-mail programs automatically add the current date after *Date*. On the *Cc* line (which stands for *carbon* or *courtesy copy*) you can type the address of anyone who is to receive a copy of the message. Remember, though, to send copies only to those people directly involved with the message. Most e-mail programs also include a line for *Bcc* (*blind carbon copy*). This sends a copy without the addressee's knowledge. Many savvy writers today use *Bcc* for the names and addresses of a list of receivers, a technique that avoids revealing the addresses to the entire group. On the subject line, identify the subject of the memo. Be sure to include enough information to be clear and compelling.

SALUTATION

How to treat the salutation is a problem. Many writers omit a salutation because they consider the message a memo. In the past, hard-copy memos were sent only to company insiders, and salutations were omitted. However, when e-mail messages travel to outsiders, omitting a salutation seems curt and unfriendly. Because the message is more like a letter, a salutation is appropriate (such as *Dear Jake; Hi, Jake; Greetings*; or just *Jake*). Including a salutation is also a visual cue to where the message begins. Many messages are transmitted or forwarded with such long headers that finding the beginning of the message can be difficult. A salutation helps, as shown in Figure 5.2. Other writers do not use a salutation; instead, they use the name of the recipient in the first sentence.

BODY

When typing the body of an e-mail message, use standard caps and lowercase characters—never all uppercase or all lowercase characters. Cover just one topic, and try to keep the total message under three screens in length. To assist you, many e-mail programs have basic text-editing features, such as cut, copy, paste, and word-wrap. However, avoid graphics, font changes, boldface, and italics unless your reader's system can handle them. Some e-mail writers use _Book Title_ to show

---

Revision helps you think through a problem, clarify a solution, and express it clearly.

E-mails contain guide words, optional salutations, and a concise and easy-to-read message.

On messages to outsiders, salutations are important to show friendliness and to indicate the beginning of the message.

FIGURE 5.2 ──────────────── • **Formatting an E-Mail Request**

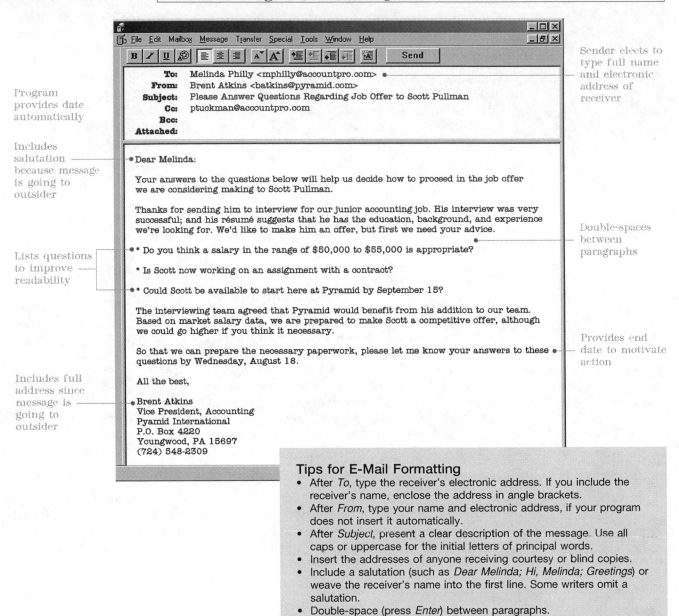

Program provides date automatically

Includes salutation because message is going to outsider

Lists questions to improve readability

Includes full address since message is going to outsider

Sender elects to type full name and electronic address of receiver

Double-spaces between paragraphs

Provides end date to motivate action

File Edit Mailbox Message Transfer Special Tools Window Help

Send

> **To:** Melinda Philly <mphilly@accountpro.com>
> **From:** Brent Atkins <batkins@pyramid.com>
> **Subject:** Please Answer Questions Regarding Job Offer to Scott Pullman
> **Cc:** ptuckman@accountpro.com
> **Bcc:**
> **Attached:**

Dear Melinda:

Your answers to the questions below will help us decide how to proceed in the job offer we are considering making to Scott Pullman.

Thanks for sending him to interview for our junior accounting job. His interview was very successful; and his résumé suggests that he has the education, background, and experience we're looking for. We'd like to make him an offer, but first we need your advice.

* Do you think a salary in the range of $50,000 to $55,000 is appropriate?

* Is Scott now working on an assignment with a contract?

* Could Scott be available to start here at Pyramid by September 15?

The interviewing team agreed that Pyramid would benefit from his addition to our team. Based on market salary data, we are prepared to make Scott a competitive offer, although we could go higher if you think it necessary.

So that we can prepare the necessary paperwork, please let me know your answers to these questions by Wednesday, August 18.

All the best,

Brent Atkins
Vice President, Accounting
Pyamid International
P.O. Box 4220
Youngwood, PA 15697
(724) 548-2309

Tips for E-Mail Formatting

- After *To*, type the receiver's electronic address. If you include the receiver's name, enclose the address in angle brackets.
- After *From*, type your name and electronic address, if your program does not insert it automatically.
- After *Subject*, present a clear description of the message. Use all caps or uppercase for the initial letters of principal words.
- Insert the addresses of anyone receiving courtesy or blind copies.
- Include a salutation (such as *Dear Melinda; Hi, Melinda; Greetings*) or weave the receiver's name into the first line. Some writers omit a salutation.
- Double-space (press *Enter*) between paragraphs.
- Do not type in all caps or in all lowercase letters.
- Include a complimentary close, your name, and full address if appropriate.

underlining and *emphasized word* to show italics. However, as more and more programs offer HTML formatting options, writers are able to use all the graphics, colors, and fonts available in their word processing program.

CLOSING LINES

E-mail messages to outsiders should include the writer's name and identification.

Writers of e-mail messages sent within organizations may omit closings and even skip their names at the end of messages. To be safe, however, always type your name. It identifies you and helps readers sort out your message within a string (thread) of messages. It also personalizes your message. For messages going to outsiders, include a closing such as *Cheers* or *All the best* followed by the writer's name and e-mail address (because some systems do not transmit your address automatically). If the recipient is unlikely to know you, it's wise to include your title, organization, full address, and telephone. Some veteran e-mail users include a *signature file* with identifying information embellished with keyboard art.

Formatting Hard-Copy Memos

Hard-copy memorandums deliver information within organizations. Although e-mail is more often used, hard-copy memos are still useful for important internal messages that require a permanent record or formality. For example, changes in procedures, official instructions, and organization reports are often prepared as hard-copy memos. Because e-mail is new and still evolving, we examined its formatting carefully in the previous paragraphs.

Hard-copy memos require less instruction because formatting is fairly standardized. Some offices use memo forms imprinted with the organization name and, optionally, the department or division names. Although the design and arrangement of memo forms vary, they usually include the basic elements of *Date, To, From*, and *Subject*. Large organizations may include other identifying headings, such as *File Number, Floor, Extension, Location*, and *Distribution*. Because of the difficulty of aligning computer printers with preprinted forms, many business writers store memo formats in their computers and call them up when preparing memos. The guide words are then printed with the message, thus eliminating alignment problems.

If no printed or stored computer forms are available, memos may be typed on company letterhead, as shown in Figure 5.3, or typed on plain paper. On a full sheet of paper, start the guide words 2 inches from the top; on a half sheet, start 1 inch from the top. Double-space and type in all caps the guide words. Align all the fill-in information 2 spaces after the longest guide word (usually *Subject*). Leave 2 blank lines between the last line of the heading and the first line of the memo. Single-space within paragraphs and double-space between paragraphs. Memos are generally formatted with side margins of 1 to 1.25 inches, or they may conform to the printed memo form. Do not justify the right margins. Research has shown that "ragged-right" margins in printed messages are easier to read.

USING E-MAIL SMARTLY AND SAFELY

Escalation in the popularity and use of e-mail staggers the imagination. Worldwide e-mail traffic is expected to triple between 2005 and 2009, from 100 million to over 300 million messages.[3] E-mail is now twice as likely as the telephone to be used to communicate at work. One survey revealed that the average employee spends about 25 percent of the workday on e-mail.[4] We have become so dependent on e-mail that 53 percent of people using it at work say that their productivity drops when they are away from it.[5]

Most of us admit that we can't get along without e-mail. But wise communicators recognize its dangers as well as its benefits. Disney's Michael Eisner gave a speech to University of Southern California students telling them of his experience and warning that thoughtless messages could cause irreparable harm.[6] Wise communicators know that their messages can travel (intentionally or unintentionally) long distances. A quickly drafted note may end up in the boss's mailbox or be forwarded to an adversary's box. Making matters worse, computers—like elephants and spurned lovers—never forget. Even erased messages can remain on network servers. Increasingly, e-mail has turned into the "smoking gun" uncovered by prosecutors to prove indelicate or even illegal intentions.[7]

E-mail has become the corporate equivalent of DNA evidence. Like forgotten land mines, damaging e-mails have been dug up to prove a prosecutor's case. For example, in the antitrust suit against Microsoft, Bill Gates squirmed when the court heard his e-mail in which he asked, "How much do we need to pay you to screw

FIGURE 5.3 ———————————— • **Hard-Copy Memo—Reply to Request**

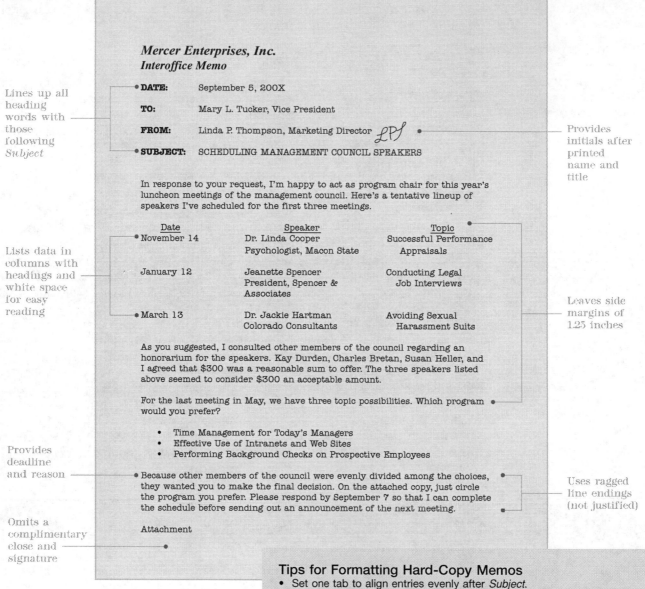

Lines up all
heading
words with
those
following
Subject

Lists data in
columns with
headings and
white space
for easy
reading

Provides
deadline
and reason

Omits a
complimentary
close and
signature

Provides
initials after
printed
name and
title

Leaves side
margins of
1.25 inches

Uses ragged
line endings
(not justified)

Mercer Enterprises, Inc.
Interoffice Memo

DATE: September 5, 200X

TO: Mary L. Tucker, Vice President

FROM: Linda P. Thompson, Marketing Director *LPT*

SUBJECT: SCHEDULING MANAGEMENT COUNCIL SPEAKERS

In response to your request, I'm happy to act as program chair for this year's
luncheon meetings of the management council. Here's a tentative lineup of
speakers I've scheduled for the first three meetings.

Date	Speaker	Topic
November 14	Dr. Linda Cooper Psychologist, Macon State	Successful Performance Appraisals
January 12	Jeanette Spencer President, Spencer & Associates	Conducting Legal Job Interviews
March 13	Dr. Jackie Hartman Colorado Consultants	Avoiding Sexual Harassment Suits

As you suggested, I consulted other members of the council regarding an
honorarium for the speakers. Kay Durden, Charles Bretan, Susan Heller, and
I agreed that $300 was a reasonable sum to offer. The three speakers listed
above seemed to consider $300 an acceptable amount.

For the last meeting in May, we have three topic possibilities. Which program
would you prefer?

• Time Management for Today's Managers
• Effective Use of Intranets and Web Sites
• Performing Background Checks on Prospective Employees

Because other members of the council were evenly divided among the choices,
they wanted you to make the final decision. On the attached copy, just circle
the program you prefer. Please respond by September 7 so that I can complete
the schedule before sending out an announcement of the next meeting.

Attachment

Tips for Formatting Hard-Copy Memos
• Set one tab to align entries evenly after *Subject*.
• Type the subject line in all caps or capitalize the initial letters of
  principal words.
• Leave 1 or 2 blank lines after the subject line.
• Single-space all but the shortest memos. Double-space between
  paragraphs.
• For full-page memos on plain paper, leave a 2-inch top margin.
• For half-page memos, leave a 1-inch top margin.
• Use 1.25-inch side margins.
• For a two-page memo, use a second-page heading with the
  addressee's name, page number, and date.
• Hardwrite your initials after your typed name.
• Place bulleted or numbered lists flush left or indent them 0.5 inches.

Netscape?" In another case banker Frank Quattrone was found guilty of obstructing justice based on an e-mail message in which he instructed employees to "clean up" their e-mail files after he learned that he was being investigated for securities irregularities.[8] More often, e-mail writers simply forget that their message is a permanent record. "It's as if people put their brains on hold when they write e-mail," said one expert. "They think that e-mail is a substitute for a phone call, and that's the danger."[9] Another observer noted that e-mail is like an electronic truth serum.[10] Writers seem to blurt out thoughts without reflecting.

Early e-mail users were encouraged to ignore stylistic and grammatical considerations. They thought that "words on the fly" required little editing or proofing. Correspondents used emoticons (such as sideways happy faces) to express their emotions. Some e-mail today is still quick and dirty. As this communication channel continues to mature, however, messages are becoming more proper, more professional, and more careful.

Getting Started

Despite its dangers and limitations, e-mail is a mainstream channel of communication. That's why it's important to take the time to organize your thoughts, compose carefully, and be concerned with correct grammar and punctuation. The following pointers will help you get off to a good start in using e-mail smartly and safely.

- **Consider composing offline.** Especially for important messages, think about using your word processing program to write offline. Then upload your message to the e-mail network. This avoids "self-destructing" (losing all your writing through some glitch or pressing the wrong key) when working online.
- **Get the address right.** E-mail addresses are sometimes complex, often illogical, and always unforgiving. Omit one character or misread the letter *l* for the number *1*, and your message bounces. Solution: Use your electronic address book for people you write to frequently. Double-check every address that you key in manually. Also be sure that you don't reply to a group of receivers when you intend to answer only one.
- **Avoid misleading subject lines.** As discussed earlier, make sure your subject line is relevant and helpful. Generic tags such as *Hi!* and *Important!* may cause your message to be deleted before it is opened.
- **Apply the top-of-screen test.** When readers open your message and look at the first screen, will they see what is most significant? Your subject line and first paragraph should convey your purpose.

Content, Tone, and Correctness

Although e-mail seems as casual as a telephone call, it's not. Because it produces a permanent record, think carefully about what you say and how you say it.

- **Be concise.** Don't burden readers with unnecessary information. Remember that monitors are small and typefaces are often difficult to read. Organize your ideas tightly.
- **Don't send anything you wouldn't want published.** Because e-mail seems like a telephone call or a person-to-person conversation, writers sometimes send sensitive, confidential, inflammatory, or potentially embarrassing messages. Beware! E-mail creates a permanent record that does not go away even when deleted. Every message is a corporate communication that can be used against you or your employer. Don't write anything that you wouldn't want your boss, your family, or a judge to read!
- **Don't use e-mail to avoid contact.** E-mail is inappropriate for breaking bad news or for resolving arguments. For example, it's improper to fire a person by e-mail. It's also not a good channel for dealing with conflict with supervisors, subordinates, or others. If there is any possibility of hurt feelings, pick up the telephone or pay the person a visit.

Because e-mail is now a mainstream communication channel, messages should be well organized, carefully composed, and grammatically correct.

Avoid sending sensitive, confidential, inflammatory, or potentially embarrassing messages because e-mail is not private.

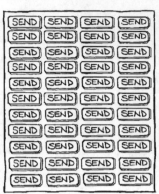

- **Care about correctness.** People are still judged by their writing, whether electronic or paper-based. Sloppy e-mail messages (with missing apostrophes, haphazard spelling, and stream-of-consciousness writing) make readers work too hard. They resent not only the information but also the writer.
- **Care about tone.** Your words and writing style affect the reader. Avoid sounding curt, negative, or domineering.
- **Resist humor and tongue-in-cheek comments.** Without the nonverbal cues conveyed by your face and your voice, humor can easily be misunderstood.

Netiquette

Although e-mail is a relatively new communication channel, a number of rules of polite online interaction are emerging.

- **Limit any tendency to send blanket copies.** Send copies only to people who really need to see a message. It is unnecessary to document every business decision and action with an electronic paper trail.
- **Never send "spam."** Sending unsolicited advertisements ("spam") either by fax or e-mail is illegal in the United States.
- **Consider using identifying labels.** When appropriate, add one of the following labels to the subject line: *Action* (action required, please respond); *FYI* (for your information, no response needed); *Re* (this is a reply to another message); *Urgent* (please respond immediately).
- **Use capital letters only for emphasis or for titles.** Avoid writing entire messages in all caps, which is like SHOUTING.
- **Don't forward without permission.** Obtain approval before forwarding a message.
- **Reduce attachments.** Because attachments may carry viruses, some receivers won't open them. Consider including short attachments within an e-mail message. If you must send a longer attachment, explain it.

Don't send blanket copies or spam, reduce attachments, and use identifying labels if appropriate.

Reading and Replying to E-Mail

The following tips can save you time and frustration when reading and answering messages:

- **Scan all messages in your inbox before replying to each individually.** Because subsequent messages often affect the way you respond, skim all messages first (especially all those from the same individual).
- **Print only when necessary.** Generally, read and answer most messages online without saving or printing. Use folders to archive messages on special topics. Print only those messages that are complex, controversial, or involve significant decisions and follow-up.

Cathy © Cathy Guisewite. Reprinted with permission of Universal Press Syndicate. All Rights Reserved.

Skim all messages before responding, paste in relevant sections, revise the subject if the topic changes, provide a clear first sentence, and never respond when angry.

- **Acknowledge receipt.** If you can't reply immediately, tell when you can (*Will respond Friday*).
- **Don't automatically return the sender's message.** When replying, cut and paste the relevant parts. Avoid irritating your recipients by returning the entire "thread" (sequence of messages) on a topic.
- **Revise the subject line if the topic changes.** When replying or continuing an e-mail exchange, revise the subject line as the topic changes.
- **Provide a clear, complete first sentence.** Avoid fragments such as *That's fine with me* or *Sounds good!* Busy respondents forget what was said in earlier messages, so be sure to fill in the context and your perspective when responding.
- **Never respond when you're angry.** Always allow some time to cool off before shooting off a response to an upsetting message. You often come up with different and better alternatives after thinking about what was said. If possible, iron out differences in person.

Personal Use

Remember that office computers are meant for work-related communication.
- **Don't use company computers for personal matters.** Unless your company specifically allows it, never use your employer's computers for personal messages, personal shopping, or entertainment.
- **Assume that all e-mail is monitored.** Employers legally have the right to monitor e-mail, and many do.

Other Smart E-Mail Practices

Depending on your messages and audience, the following tips promote effective electronic communication.

Design your messages to enhance readability, and double-check before sending.

- **Use design to improve the readability of longer messages.** When a message requires several screens, help the reader with headings, bulleted listings, side headings, and perhaps an introductory summary that describes what will follow. Although these techniques lengthen a message, they shorten reading time.
- **Consider cultural differences.** When using this borderless tool, be especially clear and precise in your language. Remember that figurative clichés (*pull up stakes, playing second fiddle*), sports references (*hit a home run, play by the rules*), and slang (*cool, stoked*) cause confusion abroad.
- **Double-check before hitting the *Send* button.** Have you included everything? Avoid the necessity of sending a second message, which makes you look careless. Use spell-check and reread for fluency before sending. It's also a good idea to check your incoming messages before sending, especially if several people are involved in a rapid-fire exchange. This helps avoid "passing"—sending out a message that might be altered depending on an incoming note.

WRITING INFORMATION AND PROCEDURE E-MAIL MESSAGES AND MEMOS

Thus far in this chapter we've reviewed the writing process, analyzed the structure and format of e-mail messages and memos, and presented a number of techniques for using e-mail smartly and safely. Now we're going to apply those techniques to two categories of messages that you can expect to be writing as a business communicator: (1) information and procedure messages and (2) request and reply messages.

Writing plans help beginners get started by providing an outline of what to include.

In this book you will be shown a number of writing plans appropriate for different messages. These plans provide a skeleton; they are the bones of a message. Writers provide the flesh. Simply plugging in phrases or someone else's words won't work. Good writers provide details and link their ideas with transitions to create fluent and meaningful messages. However, a writing plan helps you get started and gives you ideas about what to include. At first, you will probably rely on these plans considerably. As you progress, they will become less important. Later in the book, no plans are provided.

Writing Plan for Information and Procedure E-Mail Messages and Memos

- *Subject line:* Summarize the content of the message.
- *Opening:* Expand the subject line by stating the main idea concisely in a full sentence.
- *Body:* Provide background data and explain the main idea. In describing a procedure or giving instructions, use command language (*do this, don't do that*).
- *Closing:* Request action, summarize the message, or present a closing thought.

Information and procedure messages generally flow downward from management to employees.

Information and procedure messages distribute routine information, describe procedures, and deliver instructions. They typically flow downward from management to employees and relate to the daily operation of an organization. In writing these messages, you have one primary function: conveying your idea so clearly that no further explanation (return message, telephone call, or personal visit) is necessary.

You've already seen the development of a routine information message in Figure 5.1. It follows the writing plan with an informative subject line, an opening that states the purpose directly, and a body that organizes the information for maximum readability. The closing in an information message depends on what was discussed. If the message involves an action request, it should appear in the closing—not in the opening or in the body. If no action is required, the closing can summarize the message or offer some kind of closing thought.

Procedure messages must be especially clear and readable. Figure 5.4 shows the first draft of a hard-copy memo written by Troy Bell. His memo was meant to announce a new procedure for employees to follow in advertising open positions. However, the tone was negative, the explanation of the problem rambled, and the new procedure was unclear. Notice, too, that Troy's first draft told readers what they *shouldn't* do (*Do not submit advertisements for new employees directly to an Internet job bank or a newspaper*). It's more helpful to tell readers what they *should* do. Finally, Troy's memos closed with a threat instead of showing readers how this new procedure will help them.

In the revision Troy improved the tone considerably. The subject line contains a *please*, which is always pleasant to see even if one is giving an order. The subject line also includes a verb and specifies the purpose of the memo. Instead of expressing his ideas with negative words and threats, Troy revised his message to explain objectively and concisely what went wrong.

Procedures and instructions are often written in numbered steps using command language (Do this, don't do that).

Troy realized that his original explanation of the new procedure was vague. Messages explaining procedures are most readable when the instructions are broken down into numbered steps listed chronologically. Each step should begin with an action verb in the command mode. Notice in Troy's revision in Figure 5.4 that

FIGURE 5.4   • **Procedure Memo**

before revision

TO: Ruth DiSilvestro, Manager
FROM: Troy Bell, Human Resources
SUBJECT: Job Advertisement Misunderstanding •

We had no idea last month when we implemented new hiring procedures that major •
problems would result. Due to the fact that every department is now placing Internet
advertisements for new-hires individually, the difficulties occurred. This cannot continue.
Perhaps we did not make it clear at that time, but all newly hired employees who are hired
for a position should be requested through this office.

Do not submit your advertisements for new employees directly to an Internet job bank or a •
newspaper. After writing them, they should be brought to Human Resources, where they will
be centralized. You should discuss each ad with one of our counselors. Then we will place
the ad at an appropriate Internet site or other publication. If you do not follow these
guidelines, chaos will result. You may pick up applicant folders from us the day after the •
closing date in an ad.

Vague, negative
subject line

Fails to pinpoint
main idea in
opening

New procedure is
hard to follow

Uses threats instead
of showing benefits
to reader

after revision

DATE: January 5, 200x

TO: Ruth DiSilvestro, Manager

FROM: Troy Bell, Human Resources. TB

SUBJECT: Please Follow New Job Advertisement Procedure •

• To find the right candidates for your open positions as fast as possible, we're
implementing a new routine. Effective today, all advertisements for
departmental job openings should be routed through the Human Resources
Department.

A major problem resulted from the change in hiring procedures implemented
last month. Each department is placing job advertisements for new hires •
individually, when all such requests should be centralized in this office. To
process applications more efficiently, please follow this procedure:

• 1. Write an advertisement for a position in your department.

2. Bring the ad to Human Resources and discuss it with one of our counselors.

3. Let Human Resources place the ad at an appropriate Internet job bank or
submit it to a newspaper.

• 4. Pick up applicant folders from Human Resources the day following the
closing date provided in the ad.

Following these guidelines will save you work and will also enable Human •
Resources to help you fill your openings more quickly. Call Ann Edmonds at
Ext. 2505 if you have questions about this procedure.

Combines
"you" view
with main
idea in
opening

Lists easy-to-
follow steps;
starts each
with a verb

Informative,
courteous,
upbeat
subject line

Explains why
change in
procedures
is necessary

Closes by
reinforcing
benefits
to reader

numbered items begin with *Write, Bring, Let*, and *Pick up.* It's sometimes difficult to force all the steps in a procedure into this kind of command language. Troy struggled, but by trying out different wording, he finally found verbs that worked.

Why should you go to so much trouble to make lists and achieve parallelism? Because readers can comprehend what you have said much more quickly. Parallel language also makes you look professional and efficient.

In writing information and procedure messages, be careful of tone. Today's managers and team leaders seek employee participation and cooperation. These goals can't be achieved, though, if the writer sounds like a dictator or an autocrat. Avoid making accusations and fixing blame. Rather, explain changes, give reasons, and suggest benefits to the reader. Assume that employees want to contribute to the success of the organization and to their own achievement. Notice in the Figure 5.4 revision that Troy tells readers that they will save time and have their open positions filled more quickly if they follow the new procedures.

The writing of instructions and procedures is so important that we have developed a special bonus online supplement providing you with more examples and information. This online supplement extends your textbook with in-depth material including links to real businesses to show you examples of well-written procedures and instructions. To use this free supplement, go to **Guffey Xtra!** (*http://guffeyxtra .swlearning.com*) and locate *How to Write Instructions.*

> Parallel language (balanced construction) improves readability and makes the writer look professional.

WRITING REQUEST AND REPLY E-MAIL MESSAGES AND MEMOS

Business organizations require information as their fuel. To make operations run smoothly, managers and employees request information from each other and then respond to those requests. Knowing how to write those requests and responses efficiently and effectively can save you time and make you look good.

Writing Plan for Request Messages

- *Subject line:* Summarize the request and note the action desired.
- *Opening:* Begin with the request or a brief statement introducing it.
- *Body:* Provide background, justification, and details. If asking questions, list them in parallel form.
- *Closing:* Request action by a specific date. If possible, provide a reason. Express appreciation, if appropriate.

Making Requests

> Use the direct approach in routine requests for information or action, opening with the most important question, a polite command, or a brief introductory statement.

If you are requesting routine information or action within an organization, the direct approach works best. Generally, this means asking for information or making the request without first providing elaborate explanations and justifications. Remember that readers are usually thinking, "Why me? Why am I receiving this?" Readers can understand the explanation better once they know what you are requesting.

If you are seeking answers to questions, you have three options for opening the message: (1) ask the most important question first, followed by an explanation and then the other questions; (2) use a polite command (*Please answer the following questions regarding . . .*); or (3) introduce the questions with a brief statement (*Your answers to the following questions will help us . . .*).

In the body of the memo, explain and justify your request. When you must ask many questions, list them, being careful to phrase them similarly. Be courteous and friendly. In the closing include an end date (with a reason, if possible) to promote a quick response.

The e-mail message shown in Figure 5.5 requests information. The functional subject line uses a verb in noting the action desired (*Need Your Reactions to Our Casual-Dress Policy*). The reader knows immediately what is being requested. The message opens with a polite command followed by a brief explanation. Notice that the questions are highlighted with asterisks to provide the high "skim value" that is important in

FIGURE 5.5   • **Request E-Mail Message**

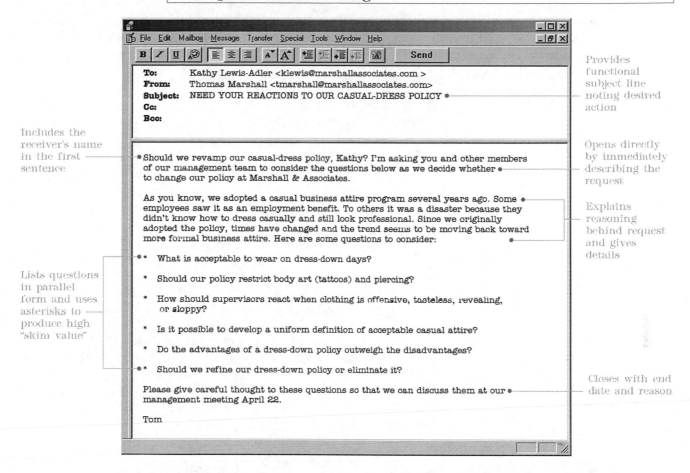

Provides functional subject line noting desired action

Includes the receiver's name in the first sentence

Opens directly by immediately describing the request

Explains reasoning behind request and gives details

Lists questions in parallel form and uses asterisks to produce high "skim value"

Closes with end date and reason

business messages. The reader can quickly see what is being asked. The message concludes with an end date and a reason. Providing an end date helps the reader know how to plan a response so that action is completed by the date given. Expressions such as *do it whenever you can* or *complete it as soon as possible* make little impression on procrastinators or very busy people. It's always wise to provide a specific date for completion. Dates can be entered on calendars to serve as reminders.

Replying to Requests

Much business correspondence reacts or responds to previous messages. When replying to an e-mail, memo, or other document, be sure to follow the three-phase writing process. Analyze your purpose and audience, collect whatever information is necessary, and organize your thoughts. Make a brief outline of the points you plan to cover following this writing plan:

Writing Plan for Replies

- *Subject line:* Summarize the main information from your reply.
- *Opening:* Start directly by responding to the request with a summary statement.
- *Body:* Provide additional information and details in a readable format.
- *Closing:* Add a concluding remark, summary, or offer of further assistance.

Overused and long-winded openers bore readers and waste their time.

Writers sometimes fall into bad habits in replying to messages. Here are some trite and long-winded openers that are best avoided:

In response to your message of the 15th . . . *(States the obvious)*

Thank you for your memo of the 15th in which you . . . *(Suggests the writer can think of nothing more original)*

I have before me your memo of the 15th in which you . . . *(Unnecessarily identifies the location of the previous message)*

Pursuant to your request of the 15th . . . *(Sounds old-fashioned)*
This is to inform you that . . . *(Delays getting to the point)*

Direct opening statements can also be cheerful and empathic.

Instead of falling into the trap of using one of the preceding shopworn openings, start directly by responding to the writer's request. If you agree to the request, show your cheerful compliance immediately. Consider these good-news openers:

Yes, we will be glad to . . . *(Sends message of approval by opening with "Yes.")*
Here are answers to the questions you asked about . . . *(Sounds straightforward, businesslike, and professional.)*
You're right in seeking advice about . . . *(Opens with two words that every reader enjoys seeing and hearing.)*
We are happy to assist you in . . . *(Shows writer's helpful nature and goodwill.)*
As you requested, I am submitting . . . *(Gets right to the point.)*

After a direct and empathic opener, provide the information requested in a logical and coherent order. If you are answering a number of questions, arrange your answers in the order of the questions. In the hard-copy memo response shown in Figure 5.3, information describing dates, speakers, and topics was listed in columns with headings. Although listing format requires more space than paragraph format, listing vastly improves readability and comprehension.

In providing additional data, use familiar words, short sentences, short paragraphs, and active-voice verbs. When alternatives exist, make them clear. Consider using graphic highlighting techniques, as shown in Figure 5.3, for both the speakers' schedules and the three program choices offered further along in the message. Imagine how much more effort would be required to read and understand the memo without the speaker list or the bulleted choices.

If further action is required, be specific in spelling it out. What may be crystal clear to you (because you have been thinking about the problem) is not always immediately apparent to a reader with limited time and interest.

SUMMING UP AND LOOKING FORWARD

E-mail messages and memorandums serve as vital channels of information for business communicators today. They use a standardized format to request and deliver information. Because e-mail is increasingly a preferred channel choice, this chapter presented many techniques for sending and receiving safe and effective e-mail messages. You learned to apply the direct strategy in writing messages that inform, request, and respond. You also learned to use bullets, numbers, and parallel form for listing information so that your messages have high "skim value." In the next chapter you will extend the direct strategy to writing direct letters and goodwill messages.

CRITICAL THINKING

1. How can the writer of a business memo or an e-mail message develop a conversational tone and still be professional? Why do e-mail writers sometimes forget to be professional?

2. What factors help you decide whether to write a memo, send an e-mail, make a telephone call, leave a voice mail message, or deliver a message in person?

3. Why are lawyers and technology experts warning companies to store, organize, and manage computer data, including e-mail and instant messages, with sharper diligence?

4. Discuss the ramifications of the following statement: *Once a memo or any other document leaves your hands, you have essentially published it.*

5. Ethical Issue: Should managers have the right to monitor the e-mail messages and instant messages of employees? Why or why not? What if employees are warned that e-mail could be monitored? If a company sets up an e-mail policy, should only in-house transmissions be monitored? Only outside transmissions?

CHAPTER REVIEW

6. List five questions you should ask yourself before writing an e-mail or memo.

7. What four parts are standard in most e-mail message and memos?

8. What techniques can writers use to improve the readability and comprehension in the body of e-mails and memos?

9. How are the structure and formatting of e-mail messages and memos similar and different?

10. Suggest at least ten pointers that you could give to a first-time e-mail user.

11. Name at least five rules of e-mail etiquette that show respect for others.

12. What are three possibilities in handling the salutation for an e-mail message?

13. What is the writing plan for an information or procedure message?
    Subject line:
    Opening:
    Body:

    Closing:

14. What is the writing plan for a request message?
    Subject line:
    Opening:
    Body:
    Closing:

15. What is the writing plan for a reply message?
    Subject line:
    Opening:
    Body:
    Closing:

WRITING IMPROVEMENT EXERCISES

Message Openers

Compare the following sets of message openers. Circle the opener that illustrates a direct opening. Be prepared to discuss the weaknesses and strengths of each.

16. A memo announcing a new procedure:
    a. It has come to our attention that increasing numbers of staff members are using instant messaging (IM) in sending business messages. We realize that IM often saves time and gets you fast responses, and we are prepared to continue to allow its use, but we have developed some specific procedures that we want you to use to make sure it is safe as well as efficient.
    b. The following new procedures for using instant messaging (IM) will enable staff members to continue to use it safely and efficiently.

17. An e-mail message inquiring about software:
    a. We are interested in your voice-recognition software that we understand allows you to dictate and copy text without touching a keyboard. We are interested in answers to a number of questions, such as the cost for a single-user license and perhaps the availability of a free trial version.
    b. Please answer the following questions about your voice-recognition software.

18. An e-mail message announcing a training program:
    a. If you would like to join our in-house leadership training program, please attend an orientation meeting June 1.
    b. For some time we have been investigating the possibility of conducting in-house leadership training courses for interested staff members.

19. An e-mail message introducing a new manager:
    a. This is a message to bring you good news. You will be pleased to learn that our long wait is over. After going without a chief for many weeks, we are finally able to welcome our new manager, Kristi Bostock, who comes to us from our Atlanta office. Please welcome her.
    b. Please welcome our new manager, Kristi Bostock, who comes from our Atlanta office.

Opening Paragraphs

The following opening paragraphs are wordy and indirect. After reading each paragraph, identify the main idea. Then, write an opening sentence that illustrates a more direct opening.

20. Our management team would like to find additional ways to improve employee motivation through recognition and reward programs. The current programs do not seem to generate an appropriate level of motivation. Because we need input from employees, we will be conducting an extensive study of all employees. But we will begin with focus groups of selected employees, and you have been selected to be part of the first focus group.

21. Customer service is an integral part of our business. That's why I was impressed when three of you came to me to ask if you might attend a seminar called "Customer Satisfaction Strategies." I understand the seminar will take place March 15 and will require you to miss a full day of work. This memo is to inform the staff that Ellen Tucker, Ryan Ho, and Sal Avila will be gone March 15 to attend the conference on customer service and satisfaction.

Bulleted and Numbered Lists

22. Use the following information to compose a list that includes an introductory statement and a numbered vertical list.
In purchasing software, be sure to follow these steps. You should tie payments to the achievement of milestones. You should also include a detailed description of all required testing. Finally, you should spell out what type of ongoing support the contract covers.

23. Use the following wordy instructions to compose a concise bulleted vertical list with an introductory statement:
To write information for a Web site, there are three important tips to follow. For one thing, you should make the formatting as simple as possible. Another thing you must do is ensure the use of strong visual prompts. Last but not least, you should limit directions that are not needed.

24. Revise the following wordy paragraph into an introduction with a list. Should you use bullets or numbers?
In writing to customers granting approval for loans, you should follow four steps that include announcing that loan approval has been granted. You should then specify the terms and limits. Next, you should remind the reader of the importance of making payments that are timely. Finally, a phone number should be provided for assistance.

25. Revise the following wordy information into a concise bulleted list with category headings:
Our attorney made a recommendation that we consider several things to avoid litigation in regard to sexual harassment. The first thing he suggested was that we take steps regarding the establishment of an unequivocal written policy prohibiting sexual harassment within our organization. The second thing we should do is make sure training sessions are held for supervisors regarding a proper work environment. Finally, some kind of official procedure for employees to lodge complaints is necessary. This procedure should include investigation of complaints.

WRITING COACH
STEP-BY-STEP DEMONSTRATION

Request E-Mail   *To help you master the entire writing process, the* Writing Coach *takes you through the problem, the writing plan, the first draft, and the final product.*

Problem

Like many office workers who sit in front of a computer all day, Trevor Williams noticed that he was spending more and more time on e-mail. As vice president of marketing at a big Midwest company, however, he was in a position to do something about it. He calls you, his assistant, into his office and says, "Some days I receive 300 or 400 messages. All this e-mail is just taking too much time! People can't get any work done around here. So I want to come up with a plan for reducing our reliance on e-mail. I think we should discuss this problem at the next supervisory committee meeting on May 10. Before the meeting, though, we need information from our people. I'd like to know how much time our employees are actually spending on e-mail. We will want to know about how many messages they are sending and receiving each day. Maybe we ought to have one day a week—let's say, Friday—that is totally e-mail free. Would that work?" Mr. Williams continues to brainstorm with you. You think you should send messages to three key supervisors asking them questions that might help solve the problem. Despite Mr. Williams' distaste for e-mail, he asks you to draft an e-mail message for him to send.

before revision

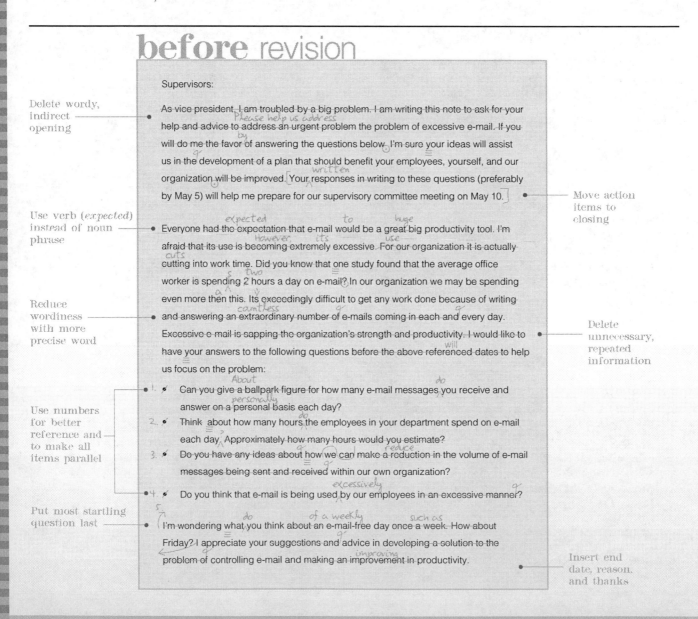

Delete wordy, indirect opening

Use verb (*expected*) instead of noun phrase

Reduce wordiness with more precise word

Use numbers for better reference and to make all items parallel

Put most startling question last

Move action items to closing

Delete unnecessary, repeated information

Insert end date, reason, and thanks

Writing Plan

SUBJECT LINE

Summarize the request and note the action desired.

Write the subject line after you finish the body of the message.

OPENING

Begin with the request or a brief statement introducing it.

The purpose of this messages is to gather information to solve the problem of excessive reliance on e-mail. The primary audience will be key supervisors who are busy but probably willing to help solve a problem. A secondary audience might be their employees. Strive to develop a "you" view. How can this request benefit the receivers?

BODY

Provide background, justification, and details. If asking questions, list them in parallel form.

Explain concisely the problem of excessive use of e-mail. For high "skim value," organize the body into a list of numbered questions. Write them in parallel form, and arrange them so that the most difficult or most startling questions are last.

CLOSING

Request action by a specific date. Provide a reason. Express appreciation.

Explain that you want responses to your questions by May 5 so that you can prepare for a supervisory committee meeting May 10.

---

after revision

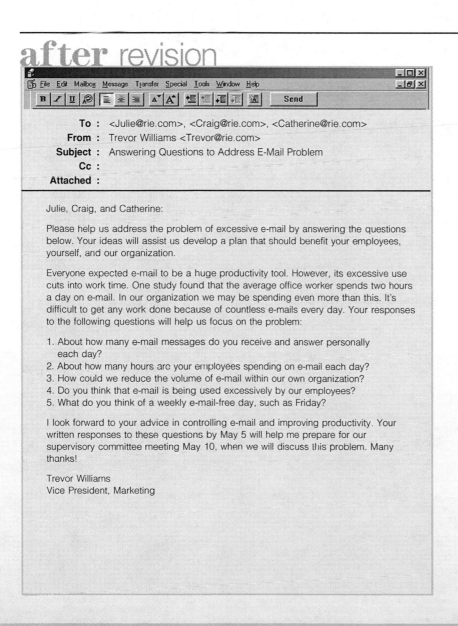

To : <Julie@rie.com>, <Craig@rie.com>, <Catherine@rie.com>
From : Trevor Williams <Trevor@rie.com>
Subject : Answering Questions to Address E-Mail Problem
Cc :
Attached :

Julie, Craig, and Catherine:

Please help us address the problem of excessive e-mail by answering the questions below. Your ideas will assist us develop a plan that should benefit your employees, yourself, and our organization.

Everyone expected e-mail to be a huge productivity tool. However, its excessive use cuts into work time. One study found that the average office worker spends two hours a day on e-mail. In our organization we may be spending even more than this. It's difficult to get any work done because of countless e-mails every day. Your responses to the following questions will help us focus on the problem:

1. About how many e-mail messages do you receive and answer personally each day?
2. About how many hours are your employees spending on e-mail each day?
3. How could we reduce the volume of e-mail within our own organization?
4. Do you think that e-mail is being used excessively by our employees?
5. What do you think of a weekly e-mail-free day, such as Friday?

I look forward to your advice in controlling e-mail and improving productivity. Your written responses to these questions by May 5 will help me prepare for our supervisory committee meeting May 10, when we will discuss this problem. Many thanks!

Trevor Williams
Vice President, Marketing

WRITING IMPROVEMENT CASES

5.1 Request E-Mail: Planning a Charity Golf Event

The following e-mail from Brad O'Bannon requests information about planning a charity golf tournament. His first draft must be revised.

Your Task. Analyze Brad's message. It suffers from many writing faults that you have studied. List its weaknesses and then outline an appropriate writing plan. If your instructor directs, revise it. Could this message benefit from category headings?

Date:	Current
To:	Gail Lobanoff <globanoff@monarch.net>
From:	Brad O'Bannon <bobannon@cox.net>
Subject:	Need Help!

The Family Outreach Center badly needs funds. We've tried other things, but now we want to try a charity golf event. In view of the fact that you have expertise in this area and since you volunteered to offer your assistance, I am writing this e-mail to pick your brain, so to speak, in regard to questions that have to do with five basic fundamentals in the process of preparation. I'm going to need your answers these areas before February 15. Is that possible? Maybe you would rather talk to me. Should I contact you?

In regard to the budget, I have no idea how to estimate costs. For example, what about administrative costs. How about marketing? And there are salaries, cell-phone rentals, copiers, and a lot of other things.

I also need help in choosing a golf course. Should it be a public course? Or a private course? Resort? One big area that I worry about is sponsors. Should I go after one big sponsor? But let's say I get Pepsi to be a sponsor. Then do I have to ban Coke totally from the scene?

Another big headache is scoring. I'll bet you can make some suggestions for tabulating the golf results. And posting them. By the way, did you see that Tiger Woods is back in the winner's circle?

I've noticed that other golf tournaments have extra events, such as a pairing party to introduce partners. Many also have an awards dinner to award prizes. Should I be planning extra events?

Brad O'Bannon
Philanthropy and Gifts Coordinator
Family Outreach Center of Miami

1. List at least five weaknesses in the preceding request e-mail.

2. Outline a writing plan for this message.
   Subject line:

   Opening:
   Body:

   Closing:

5.2 Information E-Mail: Workplace Issues

In the following e-mail message, Paul Rouse intends to inform his boss, Ceresa Rothery, about a conference he attended on the topic of workplace violence. This first draft of his information message is poorly written.

Your Task. Analyze Paul's first draft. It suffers from wordiness, poor organization, and other faults. List its weaknesses and outline an appropriate writing plan. If your instructor directs, revise it.

Date: Current

To: Ceresa Rothery <crothery@rancho.com>

From: Paul Rouse <prouse@rancho.com>

Subject: REPORT

Cc:

Ceresa:

I went to the Workplace Issues conference on November 3, as you suggested. The topic was how to prevent workplace violence, and I found it extremely fascinating. Although we have been fortunate to avoid serious incidents at our company, it's better to be safe than sorry. Because of the fact that I was the representative from our company and you asked for a report, here it is. Susan Sloan was the presenter, and she made suggestions in three categories, which I will make a summary of here.

Ms. Sloan cautioned organizations to prescreen job applicants. As a matter of fact, wise companies do not offer employment until after a candidate's background has been checked. Just the mention of a background check is sufficient and motivational enough to make some candidates head for the hills. These candidates, of course, are the ones with something to hide.

A second suggestion was that companies should become involved in the preparation of a good employee handbook that outlines what employees should do when they are suspicious of potential workplace violence. This handbook should include a way for informers to be anonymous.

A third recommendation had to do with recognizing red-flag behavior. This involves having companies train managers in the recognition of signs of potential workplace violence. What are some of the red flags? One sign is an increasing number of arguments (most of them petty) with coworkers. Another sign is extreme changes in behavior or statements that indicate the existence of depression over family or financial problems. Another sign is bullying or harassing behavior. Bringing a firearm to work or displaying an extreme fascination with firearms is another sign.

It seems to me that the best recommendation is prescreening job candidates. This is because it is most feasible. If you want me to do more research on prescreening techniques, do not hesitate to let me know. Let me know before the date of November 18 if you want me to make a report at our management meeting. Scheduled for December 3.

Did you know, by the way, that the next Workplace Issues conference is in January, and the topic is employee e-mail monitoring? That should be juicy!

Paul

1.   List at least five weaknesses in the preceding information e-mail.

2.   Outline a writing plan for this memo:
     Subject line:
     Opening:
     Body:
     Closing:

5.3 Request Memo: Choosing Your Holiday

The following memo requests a response from staff members. However, it is so poorly written that they may not know what to do.

Your Task. Analyze the message. List its weaknesses and outline an appropriate writing plan. If your instructor directs, revise it.

Date:	Current
To:	All Employees
From:	Kimberly Jackson, Human Resources
Subject:	Changing Holiday Plan

As you all know, in the past we've offered all employees 11 holidays (starting with New Year's Day in January and proceeding through Christmas Day the following December). Other companies offer similar holiday schedules.

In addition, we've given all employees one floating holiday. As you may remember, we determined that day by a companywide vote. As a result, all employees had the same day off. Now, however, we're giving consideration to a new plan that we feel would be better. This new plan involves a floating holiday that each individual employee may decide for theirself. We've given it considerable thought and decided that such a plan could definitely work. We would allow each employee to choose a day that they want. Of course, we would have to issue certain restrictions. Selections would have to be subject to our staffing needs within individual departments. For example, if everyone wanted the same day, we could not allow everyone to take it. In that case, we would allow the employee with the most seniority to have the day off.

Before we institute the new plan, though, we wanted to see what employees thought about this. Is it better to continue our current companywide uniform floating holiday? Or should we try an individual floating holiday? Please let us know what you think as soon as possible.

1. List at least five faults in this message.

2. Outline a general writing plan for this message.
   Subject line:
   Opening:
   Body:
   Closing:

ACTIVITIES AND CASES

CRITICAL THINKING   E-MAIL

5.4 Information E-Mail or Memo: What I Do on the Job

Some employees have remarked to the boss that they are working more than other employees. Your boss has decided to study the matter by asking all employees to describe exactly what they are doing. If some jobs are found to be overly demanding, your boss may redistribute job tasks or hire additional employees.

Your Task. Write a well-organized memo describing your duties, the time you spend on each task, and the skills needed for what you do. Provide enough details to make a clear record of your job. Use actual names and describe actual tasks. Describe a current or previous job. If you have not worked, report to the head of an organization to which you belong. Describe the duties of an officer or of a committee. Your boss or organization head appreciates brevity. Keep your memo under one page.

CRITICAL THINKING　　**E-MAIL**

5.5 Information E-Mail or Memo: Party Time!

Staff members in your office were disappointed that no holiday party was given last year. They don't care what kind of party it is, but they do want some kind of celebration this year.

Your Task. You have been asked to draft a memo to the office staff about a December holiday party. Decide what kind of party you would like. Include information about where the party will be held, when it is, what the cost will be, a description of the food to be served, whether guests are allowed, and whom to make reservations with.

E-MAIL

5.6 Information/Procedure E-Mail or Memo: Parking Guidelines With a Smile

As Adelle Justice, director of Human Resources, you must remind both day-shift and swing-shift employees of the company's parking guidelines. Day-shift employees must park in Lots A and B in their assigned spaces. If they have not registered their cars and received their white stickers, the cars will be ticketed.

Day-shift employees are forbidden to park at the curb. Swing-shift employees may park at the curb before 3:30 p.m. Moreover, after 3:30 p.m., swing-shift employees may park in any empty space—except those marked Tandem, Handicapped, Vanpool, Carpool, or Management. Day-shift employees may loan their spaces to other employees if they know they will not be using them.

One serious problem is lack of registration (as evidenced by white stickers). Registration is done by Employee Relations. Any car without a sticker will be ticketed. To encourage registration, Employee Relations will be in the cafeteria May 12 and 13 from 11:30 a.m. to 1:30 p.m. and from 3 p.m. to 5 p.m. to take applications and issue white parking stickers.

Your Task. Write an information/procedure e-mail or memo to employees that reviews the parking guidelines and encourages them to get their cars registered. Use listing techniques, and strive for a tone that fosters a sense of cooperation rather than resentment.

E-MAIL　　**WEB**

5.7 Information/Procedure E-Mail or Memo: Countdown to Performance Appraisal Deadline

It's time to remind all supervisory personnel that they must complete employee performance appraisals by April 15. Your boss, James Robinson, director, Human Resources, asks you to draft a procedure memo or e-mail announcing the deadline. In talking with Jim, you learn that he wants you to summarize some of the main steps in writing these appraisals. Jim says that the appraisals are really important this year because of changes in work and jobs. Many offices are installing new technologies, and some offices are undergoing reorganization. It's been a hectic year.

Jim also mentions that some supervisors will want to attend a training workshop on February 20 where they can update their skills. Supervisors who want to reserve a space at the training workshop should contact Lynn Jeffers at *ljeffers@rainco.com*. When you ask him what procedures you should include in the memo, he tells you to consult the employee handbook and pick out the most important steps.

In the handbook you find suggestions that say each employee should have a performance plan with three or four main objectives. In the appraisal the supervisor should mention three strengths the employee has, as well as three areas for improvement. One interesting comment in the handbook indicated that improvements should focus on skills, such as time management, rather than on things like being late frequently. Supervisors are supposed to use a scale of 1 to 5 to assess employees: 1 = consistently exceeds requirements; 5 = does not meet requirements at all. You think to yourself that this scale is screwy; it's certainly not like grades in school. But you can't change the scale. Finally, supervisors should meet with employees to discuss the appraisal. The completed appraisal should be sent to your office.

Your Task. Draft a memo or e-mail from James Robinson, Director, Human Resources, to all department heads, managers, and supervisors. Announce the April 15 deadline for performance appraisals. List five or six steps to be taken by supervisors in completing performance appraisals. If you need more information about writing performance appraisals, search that term on the Web. You'll find many sites with helpful advice.

E-MAIL   **TEAM**

5.8 Information E-Mail or Memo: Planning for Important Milestone

Your company hired a writing consultant to help employees improve their communication skills.

Your Task. The following poorly written message was assigned as an exercise to train your team in recognizing good and bad writing. In small groups discuss its weaknesses and then compose, either individually or as a team, an improved version.

Date:	Current
To:	All Employees
From:	Margaret Tilly, Coordinator, Employee Resources
Subject:	An Important Milestone in Your Life

We know that retirement is an important milestone in anyone's life, and we are aware that many employees do not have sufficient information that relates to the prospect of their retirement. Many employees who are approaching retirement age have come to this office wanting to talk about health, financial needs, family responsibilities, and income from outside sources and how these all relate to their retirement. It would be much easier for us to answer all these questions at once, and that is what we will try to do.

We would like to answer your questions at a series of retirement planning sessions in the company cafeteria. The first meeting is November 17. We will start at 4 p.m., which means that the company is giving you one hour of released time to attend this important session. We will meet from 4 to 6 p.m. when we will stop for dinner. We will begin again at 7 p.m. and finish at 8 p.m.

We have arranged for three speakers. They are: our company benefits supervisor, a financial planner, and a psychologist who treats retirees who have mental problems. The three sessions are planned for: November 17, November 30, and December 7.

CRITICAL THINKING   **E-MAIL**   **INFOTRAC**   **TEAM**   **WEB**

5.9 Procedure E-Mail or Memo: Should Sales Reps Use Company Cell Phones While Driving?

You saw a recent article that sent chills straight through you. A stockbroker for Smith Barney was making cold calls on his cell phone while driving. His car hit and killed a motorcyclist. The brokerage firm was sued and accused of contributing to an accident by encouraging employees to use cell phones while driving. To avoid the risk of paying huge damages awarded by an emotional jury, the brokerage firm offered the victim's family a $500,000 settlement.

As operations manager of D'anza, a hair care and skin products company, you begin to worry. You know that your company has already provided its 75 sales representatives with cell phones to help them keep in touch with home base while they are in the field.

Your Task. In teams discuss the problem. Should sales reps use their phones while driving? Is this practice allowed in your state? What happens when sales reps work in other states? Consider the possibility of ordering inexpensive hands-free devices for all sales reps. Use the Web and InfoTrac to research cell phone use, laws, and safety tips. As a team, decide on a company plan. Provide hands-free devices? Forbid calls while driving? Assume you are free to make any decision. Individually or as a team, write an e-mail or memo to sales reps explaining your decision and suggesting safety ideas. How will your decision benefit the receivers?

E-MAIL

5.10 Request E-Mail: Learning About Team Retreats

Tiptoeing gingerly across a wobbling jerrybuilt bridge of slender planks stretched between two boxes, the chief financial officer of Wells Fargo completed his task. Cheers greeted Howard Atkins as he reached the other side with a final lunge. His team of senior financial executives applauded their leader who made it across the bridge without falling off.

Atkins had pulled together a group of 73 financial executives, risk managers, accountants, and group presidents for team-building exercises on the sun-drenched lawns of a luxury hotel in Sonoma, California. The three-day retreat also provided conventional business meetings with reports and presentations. Atkins described the attendees as "very high-powered, very capable, very technically skilled, very competitive people." Yet, he was striving for an even higher level of performance. "They are very individualistic in their approach to their work," he said. "What I have been trying to do is get them to see the power of acting more like a team." And by the end of the day, he was clearly pleased with what he saw. He credits double-digit gains in Wells Fargo income and earnings in large part to the bank's people programs. "Success is more often than not a function of execution, and execution is really about people, so we invest pretty heavily in our people."

For his company's team-building exercises, Atkins chose low-stress challenges such as balancing on planks, building tents blindfolded, and stepping through complex webs of ropes. But other companies use whitewater rafting, rock walls, treetop rope bridges, and even fire pits as metaphors for the business world.

Your boss at BancFirst saw the news about Wells Fargo and is intrigued. He is understandably dubious about the value of team building that could result from a retreat. Yet, he is interested because he believes that the widespread use of electronic technology is reducing personal contact. He asks you to have the Human Resources Department investigate.[11]

Your Task. As assistant to the president, draft an e-mail to Charlotte Evers, Manager, Human Resources. Ask her to investigate the possibility of a retreat for BancFirst. Your message should include many questions for her to answer. Include an end date and a reason.

CRITICAL THINKING — **INFOTRAC** — **E-MAIL** — **TEAM**

5.11 Reply Memo or E-Mail: Office Romances Off Limits?

Where can you find the hottest singles scene today? Some would say in your workplace. Because people are working long hours and have little time for outside contacts, relationships often develop at work. Estimates suggest that one third to one half of all romances start at work. Your boss is concerned about possible problems resulting from relationships at work. What happens if a relationship between a superior and subordinate results in perceived favoritism? What happens if a relationship results in a nasty breakup? Your boss would like to simply ban all relationships among employees. But that's not likely to work. He asks you, his assistant, to learn what guidelines could be established regarding office romances.

Your Task. Using InfoTrac, read Timothy Bland's "Romance in the Workplace: Good Thing or Bad?" (Article No. A66460590). From this article select four or five suggestions that you could make to your boss in regard to protecting an employer. Why is it necessary for a company to protect itself? Discuss your findings and reactions with your team. Individually or as a group, submit your findings and reactions in a well-organized, easy-to-read e-mail or memo to your boss (your instructor). You may list main points from the article, but use your own words to write the message.

CRITICAL THINKING — **E-MAIL** — **TEAM**

5.12 Reply Memo or E-Mail: One Sick Day Too Many

As director of Human Resources at a midsized insurance company, you received an inquiry from Suzette Chase, who is supervisor of Legal Support. It seems that one of Suzette's veteran employees recently implemented a four-day workweek for herself. On the fifth morning, the employee calls in with some crisis or sickness that makes it impossible for her to get to work. Suzette asks for your advice in how to handle this situation.

In the past you've told supervisors to keep a written record (a log) of each absence. This record should include the financial and productive impact of the absence. It should include a space where the employee can include her comments and signature. You've found that a written document always increases the significance of the event. You've also told supervisors that they must be objective and professional. It's difficult, but they should not personalize the situation.

Occasionally, of course, an absence is legitimate. Supervisors must know what is unavoidable and what is a lame excuse. In other words, they must know how to separate reasons from excuses. Another thing to consider is how the employee reacts when approached. Is her attitude sincere, or does she automatically become defensive?

You also tell supervisors that "if they talk the talk, they must walk the walk." In other words, they must follow the same policies that are enforced. The best plan, of course, is to clearly define what is and is not acceptable attendance policy and make sure every new-hire is informed.

Your Task. In teams discuss what advice to give to Suzette Chase regarding her habitually absent worker. Why is a log important? What other suggestions can you make? How should you conclude this message? Individually or in teams, write a well-organized reply memo or e-mail message to Suzette Chase, Supervisor, Legal Support. Remember that bulleted items improve readability.

`INFOTRAC`   `E-MAIL`   `TEAM`

5.13 Reply E-Mail: Managing the Mountains of E-Mail

E-mail has become an essential part of our business lives. Yet workers throughout the country may be losing hours from each business day because of it. Some are distracted from work and waste valuable time on meaningless communications, says Dr. Mark Langemo, records management author and expert. In an article titled "11 Practical Strategies for Managing E-Mail" (InfoTrac Article No. A111112220), Dr. Langemo tells how companies can manage e-mail more efficiently and reduce their legal vulnerability. The vice president of your company has been complaining that e-mail is out of control. He asks you to be on the lookout for any ideas he should present to management for dealing with the problem.

Your Task: Using InfoTrac, study the article. You believe that some of the suggestions would certainly work for your company. You decide to discuss them with your team. Decide which of the suggestions are most appropriate, and organize them into a set of procedures. What should be done first? Some of the suggestions could be combined with others. Once your team agrees on a set of procedures, write an e-mail to Vice President Stanton Childress (or your instructor). In your own words, list the most significant strategies and explain each briefly.

`E-MAIL`   `TEAM`   `WEB`

5.14 Reply E-Mail or Memo: Cross-Cultural Dilemma

The Air Force's highest-ranking female fighter pilot, Lt. Col. Martha McSally, was unhappy about being required to wear neck-to-toe robes in Saudi Arabia when she's off base. She filed a federal lawsuit seeking to overturn the policy that requires female servicewomen to wear such conservative clothing even when they are off base.

After seeing an article about this in the newspaper, your boss was concerned about sending female engineers to Saudi Arabia. Your company has been asked to submit a proposal to develop telecommunications within that country, and some of the company's best staff members are female. If your company wins the contract, it will undoubtedly need women to be in Saudi Arabia to complete the project. Because your boss knows little about the country, he asks you, his assistant, to do some research to find out what is appropriate business dress.

Your Task. Visit two or three Web sites and learn about dress expectations in Saudi Arabia. Is Western-style clothing acceptable for men? For women? Are there any clothing taboos? Should guest workers be expected to dress like natives? In teams discuss your findings. Individually or collectively, prepare a memo or e-mail addressed to J. E. Rivers, your boss. Summarize your most significant findings.

`E-MAIL`

5.15 Reply Memo or E-Mail: Scheduling Appointments to Interview a New Project Manager

You're frustrated! Your boss, Paul Rosenberg, has scheduled three appointments to interview applicants for the position of project manager. All of these appointments are for Thursday, May 5. However, he now must travel to Atlanta on that weekend. He asks you to reschedule all the appointments for one week later. He also wants a brief summary of the background of each candidate.

Despite your frustration, you call each person and are lucky to arrange these times. Carol Chastain, who has been a project manager for nine years with Piedmont Corporation, agrees to come at 10:30 a.m. Richard Emanuel, who is a systems analyst and a consultant to many companies, will come at 11:30. Lara Lee, who has an M.A. degree and six years of experience as senior project coordinator at High Point Industries, will come at 9:30 a.m. You're wondering whether Mr. Rosenberg forgot to include Hilary Iwu, operations personnel officer, in these interviews. Ms. Iwu usually is part of the selection process.

Your Task. Write an e-mail or memo to Mr. Rosenberg including all the vital information he needs.

`CRITICAL THINKING`   `E-MAIL`   `INFOTRAC`   `TEAM`

5.16 Reply E-Mail: Reaching Consensus Regarding Casual-Dress Policy

Casual dress in professional offices has been coming under attack. Your boss, Kathy Lewis-Adler, received the e-mail shown in Figure 5.5. She thinks it would be a good assignment for her group of management trainees to help her respond to that message. She asks your team to research answers to the first five questions in CEO Thomas Marshall's message. She doesn't expect you to answer the final question, but any information you can supply to the first questions would help her shape a response.

Marshall & Associates is a public CPA firm with a staff of 120 CPAs, bookkeepers, managers, and support personnel. Located in downtown Pittsburgh, the plush offices in One Oxford Center overlook the Allegheny River and the North Shore. The firm performs general accounting and audit services as well as tax planning and preparation. Accountants visit clients in the field and also entertain them in the downtown office.

Your Task. Decide whether the entire team will research each question in Figure 5.5 or whether team members will be assigned certain questions. Collect information, discuss it, and reach consensus on what you will report to Ms. Lewis-Adler. Write a concise, one-page response from your team. Your goal is to inform, not persuade. Remember that you represent management, not students or employees.

INFOTRAC   TEAM   WEB

5.17 Reply Memo: Squawking About a Company E-Mail Policy

At first, he couldn't figure it out. The IS (Information Systems) network manager at Lionel Trains in Chesterfield, Michigan, fretted that his company would have to upgrade its Internet connection because operations were noticeably slower than in the past. Upon checking, however, he discovered that extensive recreational Web surfing among employees was the real reason for the slowdown. Since the company needed a good policy regulating the use of e-mail and the Internet, he assigned your team the task of investigating existing policies. Your team leader, Rick Rodriquez, who has quite a sense of humor, said, "Adopting an Internet policy is a lot like hosting a convention of pigeons. Both will result in a lot of squawking, ruffled feathers, and someone getting dumped on." Right! No one is going to like having e-mail and Internet use restricted. It is, indeed, a dirty job, but someone has to do it.

Your Task. Working individually, locate examples or models of company e-mail and Internet policies. Use InfoTrac and the Web trying variations of the search term "Company E-Mail Policy." Print any helpful material. Then meet as a group and select six to eight major topics that you think should be covered in a company policy. Your investigation will act as a starting point in the long process of developing a policy that provides safeguards but is not overly restrictive. You are not expected to write the policy at this time. But you could attach copies of anything interesting. Your boss would especially like to know where he could see or purchase model company policies. Send a reply memo to Rick Rodriquez, your team leader.

VIDEO RESOURCES

This important chapter offers two learning videos.

Video Library 1, *Building Workplace Communication Skills: Smart E-Mail Messages and Memos Advance Your Career.* Watch this chapter-specific video for a demonstration of how to use e-mail skillfully and safely. You'll better understand the writing process in relation to composing messages. You'll also see tips for writing messages that advance your career instead of sinking it.

Video Library 2, *Bridging the Gap: Innovation, Learning, and Communication: A Study of Yahoo.* This video familiarizes you with managers and inside operating strategies at the Internet company Yahoo. After watching the film, assume the role of assistant to John Briggs, senior producer, who appeared in the video. John has just received a letter asking for permission from another film company to use Yahoo offices and personnel in an educational video, similar to the one you just saw.

John wants you to draft a message for him to send to the operations manager, Ceci Lang, asking for permission for VX Studios to film. VX says it needs about 15 hours of filming time and would like to interview four or five managers as well as founders David Filo and Jerry Yang. VX would need to set up its mobile studio van in the parking lot and would need permission to use advertising film clips. Although VX hopes to film in May, it is flexible about the date. John Briggs reminds you that Yahoo has participated in a number of films in the past two years, and some managers are complaining that they can't get their work done.

Your Task. After watching the video, write a memo or e-mail request message to Ceci Lang, operations manager, asking her to allow VX Studios to film at Yahoo. Your message should probably emphasize the value of these projects in enhancing Yahoo's image among future users. Supply any other details you think are necessary to create a convincing request memo that will win authorization from Ceci Lang to schedule this filming.

• GRAMMAR/MECHANICS CHECKUP—5

Prepositions and Conjunctions

Review Sections 1.18 and 1.19 in the Grammar Review section of the Grammar/ Mechanics Handbook. Then study each of the following statements. Write *a* or *b* to indicate the sentence in which the idea is expressed more effectively. Also record the number of the G/M principle illustrated. When you finish, compare your responses with those provided. If your answers differ, study carefully the principles shown in parentheses.

b _____ (1.18a)   **Example**   a. When did you graduate high school?
                                            b. When did you graduate from high school?

_____   1. a. Your iPod was more expensive than mine.
                       b. Your iPod was more expensive then mine.

_____   2. a. Don't you hate when your inbox is filled with spam?
                       b. Don't you hate it when your inbox is filled with spam?

_____   3. a. If the company called you, than it must be looking at your résumé.
                       b. If the company called you, then it must be looking at your résumé.

_____   4. a. Ethnocentrism is when you believe your culture is best.
                       b. Ethnocentrism involves the belief that your culture is best.

_____   5. a. Business messages should be clear, correct, and written with conciseness.
                       b. Business messages should be clear, correct, and concise.

_____   6. a. What type computer monitor do you prefer?
                       b. What type of computer monitor do you prefer?

_____   7. a. Do you know where the meeting is at?
                       b. Do you know where the meeting is?

_____   8. a. Did you send an application to the headquarters in Cincinnati or to the branch in St. Louis?
                       b. Did you apply to the Cincinnati headquarters or the St. Louis branch?

_____   9. a. That Hollywood actor appeared in movies, plays, and television.
                       b. That Hollywood actor appeared in movies, in plays, and on television.

_____   10. a. She had a great interest, as well as a profound respect for, historical homes.
                        b. She had a great interest in, as well as a profound respect for, historical homes.

_____   11. a. Volunteers should wear long pants, bring gloves, and sunscreen should be applied.
                        b. Volunteers should wear long pants, bring gloves, and apply sunscreen.

_____   12. a. His PowerPoint presentation was short like we hoped it would be.
                        b. His PowerPoint presentation was short as we hoped it would be.

_____   13. a. An ethics code is where a set of rules spells out appropriate behavior standards.
                        b. An ethics code is a set of rules spelling out appropriate behavior standards.

_____   14. a. Please keep the paper near the printer.
                        b. Please keep the paper near to the printer.

_____   15. a. A behavioral interview question is when the recruiter says, "Tell me about a time. . . ."
                        b. A behavioral interview question is one in which the recruiter says, "Tell me about a time. . . ."

● GRAMMAR/MECHANICS CHALLENGE—5

The following memo has faults in grammar, punctuation, spelling, capitalization, number form, repetition, wordiness, and other problems. Correct the errors with standard proofreading marks (see Appendix B) or revise the message online at **Guffey Xtra!**

DATE: March 2, 200x

TO: Department Heads, Managers, and Supervisors

FROM: James Robbins, Director, Human Resources   *JR*

SUBJECT: Submitting Appraisals of Performance by April 15th

Please be informed that performance appraisals for all you're employees' are due, before April 15th. These appraisal are esspecially important and essential this year. Because of job changes, new technologys and because of office re-organization.

To complete your performance appraisals in the most effective way, you should follow the procedures described in our employee handbook, let me briefly make a review of those procedures;

1. Be sure each and every employee has a performance plan with 3 or 4 main objective.

2. For each objective make an assessment of the employee on a scale of 5 (consistently excedes requirements) to 0 (does not meet requirements at all.

3. You should identify 3 strengths that he brings to the job.

4. Name 3 skills that he can improve. These should pertain to skills such as Time Management rather then to behaviors such as habitual lateness.

5. The employee should be met with to discuss his appraisal.

6. Finish the appraisal and send the completed appraisal to this office.

We look upon appraisals like a tool for helping each worker assess his performance. And enhance his output. If you would like to discuss this farther, please do not hessitate to call me.

COMMUNICATION WORKSHOP
ETHICS

WHOSE COMPUTER
IS IT ANYWAY?

Many companies provide their employees with computers and Internet access. Should employees be able to use those computers for online shopping, personal messages, and personal work, as well as to listen to music and play games?

But It's Harmless

The Wall Street Journal reports that many office workers have discovered that it's far easier to shop online than to race to malls and wait in line. To justify her Web shopping at work, one employee, a recent graduate, says, "Instead of standing at the water cooler gossiping, I shop online." She went on to say, "I'm not sapping company resources by doing this."

Some online office shoppers say that what they're doing is similar to making personal phone calls. So long as they don't abuse the practice, they see no harm. Besides, shopping at the office is far faster than shopping from slow dial-up connections at home. Marketing director David Krane justifies his online shopping by explaining that his employer benefits because he is more productive when he takes minibreaks. "When I need a break, I just pull up a Web page and just browse," he says. "Ten minutes later, I'm all refreshed, and I can go back to business-plan writing."

Companies Cracking Down

Employers, however, do not approve of the increasing use of company networks for personal online activities. A study of business organizations found that one in five companies has terminated an employee for e-mail infractions.[12] UPS discovered an employee running a personal business from his office computer. Lockheed Martin fired an employee who disabled its entire company network for six hours because of an e-mail message heralding a holiday event that the worker sent to 60,000 employees. Employees who use company Internet connections to download large documents—especially MP3 music—gobble up a huge amount of bandwidth.[13]

Attorney Carole O'Blenes thinks that companies should begin cracking down. Online shopping generates junk e-mail that could cause the company's server to crash. And what about productivity? "Whether they're checking their stocks, shopping, or doing research for their upcoming trip to Spain," she says, "that's time diverted from doing business."[14]

What's Reasonable?

Some companies try to enforce a "zero tolerance" policy, prohibiting any personal use of company equipment. Ameritech Corporation specifically tells employees that "computers and other company equipment are to be used only to provide service to customers and for other business purposes." Companies such as Boeing, however, allow employees to use faxes, e-mail, and the Internet for personal reasons. But Boeing sets guidelines. Use has to be of "reasonable duration and frequency" and can't cause "embarrassment to the company."[15] Strictly prohibited are chain letters, obscenity, and political and religious solicitation.

Career Application. As an administrative assistant at Texas Technologies in Fort Worth, you have just received an e-mail from your boss asking for your opinion. It seems that many employees have been shopping online; one person actually received four personal packages from UPS in one morning. Although reluctant to do so, management is considering installing monitoring software that not only tracks Internet use but also blocks pornography, hate, and game sites.

Your Task

- In teams or as a class, discuss the problem of workplace abuse of e-mail and the Internet. Should full personal use be allowed?
- Are computers and their links to the Internet similar to other equipment such as telephones?
- Should employees be allowed to access the Internet for personal use if they use their own private e-mail accounts?
- Should management be allowed to monitor all Internet use?
- Should employees be warned if e-mail is to be monitored?
- What specific reasons can you give to support an Internet crackdown by management?
- What specific reasons can you give to oppose a crackdown?

Decide whether you support or oppose the crackdown. Explain your views in an e-mail or a memo to your boss, Arthur W. Rose, *awrose@txtech.com*.

CHAPTER 6

DIRECT LETTERS AND GOODWILL MESSAGES

OBJECTIVES

- Write direct requests for information and action.
- Write direct claims.
- Write direct responses to information requests.
- Write adjustment letters.
- Write letters of recommendation.
- Write goodwill messages.

"A good business letter can get you a job interview, get you off the hook, or get you money. It's totally asinine to blow your chances of getting whatever you want—with a business letter that turns people off instead of turning them on.[1]"

Malcolm Forbes,
Publisher and Founder,
Forbes Magazine

WRITING EFFECTIVE DIRECT BUSINESS LETTERS

Publisher Malcolm Forbes understood the power of business letters. They can get you anything you want if you can write letters that turn people on instead of off. This chapter teaches you how to turn readers on with effective business letters and goodwill messages. Most of these messages travel outside an organization.

Although e-mail is incredibly successful for both internal and external communication, many important messages still call for letters. Business letters are important when a permanent record is required, when formality is necessary, and when a message is sensitive and requires an organized, well-considered presentation. In this book we'll divide messages into three groups: (1) direct letters communicating straightforward requests, replies, and goodwill messages in Chapter 6; (2) persuasive messages including sales pitches in Chapter 7; and (3) negative messages delivering refusals and bad news in Chapter 8.

This chapter concentrates on direct letters through which we conduct everyday business and convey goodwill to outsiders. Such letters go to suppliers, government agencies, other businesses, and most important, customers. Customer letters receive

> Letters communicate with outsiders and produce a formal record.

a high priority because these messages encourage product feedback, project a favorable image of the company, and promote future business. You'll learn to write direct requests for information and action, direct claims, direct responses to information requests, adjustment letters, letters of recommendation, and goodwill messages.

DIRECT REQUESTS FOR INFORMATION AND ACTION

The content of a message and its anticipated effect on the reader determine the strategy you choose.

Like memos, letters are easiest to write when you have a plan to follow. The plan for letters, just as for memos, is fixed by the content of the message and its expected effect on the receiver. Many of your messages will request information or action. Although the specific subject of each inquiry may differ, the similarity of purpose in direct requests enables writers to use the following writing plan:

Writing Plan for Direct Requests for Information or Action

- *Opening:* Ask the most important question first or express a polite command.
- *Body:* Explain the request logically and courteously. Ask other questions if necessary.
- *Closing:* Request a specific action with an end date, if appropriate, and show appreciation.

Opening Directly

Readers find the openings and closings of letters most interesting and often read them first.

The most emphatic positions in a letter are the openings and closings. Readers tend to look at them first. The writer, then, should capitalize on this tendency by putting the most significant statement first. The first sentence of a direct request is usually a question or a polite command. It should not be an explanation or justification, unless resistance to the request is expected. When the information requested is likely to be forthcoming, immediately tell the reader what you want. This saves the reader's time and may ensure that the message is read. A busy executive skims the mail, quickly reading subject lines and first sentences only. That reader may grasp your request rapidly and act on it. A request that follows a lengthy explanation, on the other hand, may never be found.

A letter inquiring about hotel accommodations, shown in Figure 6.1, begins immediately with the most important idea. Can the hotel provide meeting rooms and accommodations for 250 people? Instead of opening with an explanation of who the writer is or how the writer happens to be writing this letter, the letter begins more directly.

Begin an information request letter with the most important question or a summarizing statement.

If your request involves several questions, you could open with a polite request, such as *Will you please answer the following questions about* . . . . Note that although this request sounds like a question, it's actually a disguised command. Because you expect an action rather than a reply, punctuate this polite command with a period instead of a question mark. If you use a period, however, some readers will think you have made a punctuation error. To avoid this punctuation problem, just omit *Will you* and start with *Please answer*, as the writer did in Figure 6.1.

Providing Details in the Body

The body of a request letter may contain an explanation or a list of questions.

The body of a letter that requests information should provide necessary details. Remember that the quality of the information obtained from a request letter depends on the clarity of the inquiry. If you analyze your needs, organize your ideas, and frame your request logically, you are likely to receive a meaningful answer that doesn't require a follow-up message. Whenever possible, itemize the information to improve readability. Notice that the questions in Figure 6.1 are bulleted, and they are parallel. That is, they use the same balanced construction.

FIGURE 6.1 • **Direct Request Letter**

Letterhead

Dateline

Inside address

Salutation

Body

Complimentary close

Author's name and identification

Reference initials

DCC 958 Alum Creek Drive Columbus, OH 43208   PHONE: (614) 455-3201
                                                         FAX: (614) 455-6621 WEB: www.dcc.com
Digital Communication Corporation

October 14, 200x

Mr. Dennis Purdy, Manager
MGM Grand Hotel and Casino
3799 Las Vegas Boulevard South
Las Vegas, NV 89109

Dear Mr. Purdy:

Can the MGM Grand Hotel provide meeting rooms and accommodations for
about 250 DCC sales representatives from May 25 through May 29?

Your hotel received strong recommendations because of its excellent resort and
conference facilities. Our spring sales conference is scheduled for next May, and
I am collecting information for our planning committee. Please answer these
additional questions regarding the MGM Grand:

• Does the hotel have a banquet room that can seat 250?

• Do you have at least four smaller meeting rooms, each to accommodate a
  maximum of 75?

• What kinds of computer facilities are available for electronic presentations?

• What is the nearest airport, and do you provide transportation to and from it?

Answers to these questions and any other information you can provide will help
us decide which conference facility to choose. Your response before November 15
would be most appreciated since our planning committee meets November 19.

Sincerely yours,

Carol A. Allen

Carol A. Allen
Corporate Travel Department

CAA:gdr

Tips for Formatting Letters
• Start the date 2 inches from the top or 1 blank line below the
  letterhead.
• For block style, begin all lines at the left margin.
• Leave side margins of 1 to 1½ inches depending on the length of the
  letter.
• Single-space the body and double-space between paragraphs.
• Bulleted items may appear flush left or indented.

Closing With Appreciation and an Action Request

The ending of a request letter should tell the reader what you want done and when.

Use the final paragraph to ask for specific action, to set an end date if appropriate, and to express appreciation. As you learned in working with memos, a request for action is most effective when you supply an end date and reason for that date, as shown in Figure 6.1.

It's always appropriate to end a request letter with appreciation for the action taken, but try to do so in a fresh and efficient manner. For example, you could hook your thanks to the end date (*Thanks for responding before November 15 when we must make a decision*). You might connect your appreciation to a statement developing reader benefits (*We are grateful for the information you will provide because it will help us improve our service to you*). You could also describe briefly how the information will help you (*I appreciate this information that will enable me to . . .*). When possible make it easy for the reader to comply with your request (*Note your answers on this sheet and return it in the postage-paid envelope* or *Here's my e-mail address so that you can reach me quickly*). Avoid cliché endings such as *Thank you for your cooperation*. Your appreciation will sound most sincere if you avoid mechanical, tired expressions.

DIRECT CLAIMS

Direct claims are written by customers to identify and correct a wrong.

In business many things can go wrong—promised shipments are late, warranted goods fail, or service is disappointing. When you as a customer must write to identify or correct a wrong, the letter is called a *claim*. Straightforward claims are those to which you expect the receiver to agree readily. But even these claims often require a letter. While your first action may be a telephone call or a visit to submit your claim, you may not get the results you seek. Written claims are often taken more seriously, and they also establish a record of what happened. Claims that require persuasion are presented in Chapter 7. In this chapter you'll learn to apply the following writing plan for a straightforward claim that uses a direct approach.

Writing Plan for Direct Claims

- *Opening:* Describe clearly the desired action.
- *Body:* Explain the nature of the claim, tell why the claim is justified, and provide details regarding the action requested.
- *Closing:* End courteously with a goodwill statement that summarizes your action request.

Customers who call to complain may not reach the right person at the best time. To register a serious claim, always write a letter. A letter creates a paper trail and is taken more seriously than a telephone call. Use the direct strategy for straightforward claims.

Opening With a Clear Statement

Claim letters open with a clear problem statement or with an explanation of the action necessary to solve the problem.

When you, as a customer, have a legitimate claim, you can expect a positive response from a company. Smart businesses want to hear from their customers. They know that retaining a customer is far less costly than recruiting a new customer. That's why you should open a claim letter with a clear statement of the problem or with the action you want the receiver to take. You might expect a replacement, a refund, a new order, credit to your account, correction of a billing error, free repairs, free inspection, or cancellation of an order. When the remedy is obvious, state it immediately (*Please send us 25 Sanyo digital travel alarm clocks to replace the Sanyo analog travel alarm clocks sent in error with our order shipped January 4*). When the remedy is less obvious, you might ask for a change in policy or procedure or simply for an explanation (*Because three of our employees with confirmed reservations were refused rooms September 16 in your hotel, please clarify your policy regarding reservations and late arrivals*).

Explaining and Justifying in the Body

Providing details without getting angry improves the effectiveness of a claim letter.

In the body of a claim letter, explain the problem and justify your request. Provide the necessary details so that the difficulty can be corrected without further correspondence. Avoid becoming angry or trying to fix blame. Bear in mind that the person reading your letter is seldom responsible for the problem. Instead, state the facts logically, objectively, and unemotionally. Let the reader decide on the causes. Include copies of all pertinent documents such as invoices, sales slips, catalog descriptions, and repair records. (By the way, be sure to send copies and NOT your originals, which could be lost.) When service is involved, cite names of individuals spoken to and dates of calls. Assume that a company honestly wants to satisfy its customers—because most do. When an alternative remedy exists, spell it out (*If you are unable to send 25 Sanyo digital travel alarm clocks immediately, please credit our account now and notify us when they become available*).

Concluding With an Action Request

Close a claim letter with a summary of the action requested and a courteous goodwill statement.

End a claim letter with a courteous statement that promotes goodwill and summarizes your action request. If appropriate, include an end date (*We realize that mistakes in ordering and shipping sometimes occur. Because we've enjoyed your prompt service in the past, we hope that you will be able to send us the Sanyo digital travel alarm clocks by January 15*). Finally, in making claims, act promptly. Delaying claims makes them appear less important. Delayed claims are also more difficult to verify. By taking the time to put your claim in writing, you indicate your seriousness. A written claim starts a record of the problem, should later action be necessary. Be sure to keep a copy of your letter.

When Keith Krahnke received a statement showing a charge for a three-year service warranty that he did not purchase, he was furious. He called the store but failed to get satisfaction to his complaint. Then he decided to write. You can see the first draft of his direct claim letter in Figure 6.2. This draft gave him a chance to vent his anger, but it accomplished little else. The tone was belligerent, and it assumed that the company intentionally mischarged him. Furthermore, it failed to tell the reader how to remedy the problem. The revision, also shown in Figure 6.2, tempered the tone, described the problem objectively, and provided facts and figures. Most important, it specified exactly what Keith wanted to be done.

Notice in Figure 6.2 that Keith used the personal business letter style, which is appropriate for you to use in writing personal messages. Your return address, but not your name, appears above the date. Keith used modified block style, in which the return address, date, and closing lines start at the center. Full block style, however, is also appropriate for personal business letters.

FIGURE 6.2   • **Direct Claim Letter**

before revision

Dear Good Vibes:

You call yourselves Good Vibes, but all I'm getting from your service are bad • ——— Sounds angry; jumps
vibes! I'm furious that you have your salespeople slip in unwanted service   to conclusions
warranties to boost your sales.

When I bought my Panatronic DVR from Good Vibes, Inc., in August, I
specifically told the salesperson that I did NOT want a three-year service
warranty. But there it is on my Visa statement this month! You people have • ——— Forgets that mistakes
obviously billed me for a service I did not authorize. I refuse to pay this   happen
charge.

How can you hope to stay in business with such fraudulent practices? I was
expecting to return this month and look at MP3 players, but you can be sure • ——— Fails to suggest
I'll find an honest dealer this time.   solution

                    Sincerely,

after revision

                                        1201 Lantana Court   Personal
                                        Lake Worth, FL 33461 • ——————— business letter
                                        September 3, 200x   style

            Mr. Sam Lee, Customer Service
            Good Vibes, Inc.
            2003 53rd Street
            West Palm Beach, FL 33407

            Dear Mr. Lee:

            Please credit my Visa account to correct an erroneous charge of $299. • ——— States simply
                                                                                      and clearly
Explains   what to do
objectively ——— • On August 1 I purchased a Panatronic DVR from Good Vibes, Inc. Although
what went   the salesperson discussed a three-year extended warranty with me, I
wrong   decided against purchasing that service for $299. However, when my credit
                card statement arrived this month, I noticed an extra $299 charge from • ——— Doesn't blame
                Good Vibes, Inc. I suspect that this charge represents the warranty I   or accuse
Documents ——— • declined. Enclosed is a copy of my sales invoice along with my Visa
facts   statement on which I circled the charge.

            Please authorize a credit immediately and send a copy of the transaction to   Summarizes
            me at the above address. I'm enjoying all the features of my Panatronic   request and
            DVR and would like to be shopping at Good Vibes for an MP3 player shortly.• ——— courteously
                                                                                            suggests
                        Sincerely,   continued
                                                                                            business once
                        Keith Krahnke   problem is
                        Keith Krahnke   resolved

            Enclosure

REPLIES TO INFORMATION REQUESTS

Before responding to requests, gather facts, check figures, and seek approval if necessary.

Often, your messages will respond favorably to requests for information or action. A customer wants information about a product. A supplier asks to arrange a meeting. Another business inquires about one of your procedures. But before responding to any inquiry, be sure to check your facts and figures carefully. Any letter written on company stationery is considered a legally binding contract. If a policy or procedure needs authorization, seek approval from a supervisor or executive before writing the letter. In complying with requests, you'll want to apply the same direct pattern you used in making requests.

Writing Plan for Information Replies

- *Subject line:* Identify previous correspondence and/or refer to the main idea.
- *Opening:* Deliver the most important information first.
- *Body:* Arrange information logically, explain and clarify it, provide additional information if appropriate, and build goodwill.
- *Closing:* End pleasantly.

Summarizing in the Subject Line

Use the subject line to identify previous correspondence and the main idea.

An information response letter might contain a subject line, which helps the reader recognize the topic immediately. Knowledgeable business communicators use a subject line to refer to earlier correspondence or to summarize the main idea. Notice in Figure 6.3 that the subject line identifies the subject completely (*Your July 12 Inquiry About WorkZone Software*). A subject line helps the reader recognize the topic immediately.

Opening Directly

In the first sentence of an information response, deliver the information the reader wants. Avoid wordy, drawn-out openings (*I have before me your letter of July 12, in which you request information about . . .*). More forceful and more efficient is an opener that answers the inquiry (*Here is the information you wanted about . . .*). When agreeing to a request for action, announce the good news promptly (*Yes, I will be happy to speak to your business communication class on the topic of . . .*).

Arranging Information Logically

A good way to answer questions is to number or bullet each one.

When answering a group of questions or providing considerable data, arrange the information logically and make it readable by using lists, tables, headings, boldface, italics, or other graphic devices. When customers or prospective customers inquire about products or services, your response should do more than merely supply answers. You'll also want to promote your organization and products. Be sure to present the promotional material with attention to the "you" view and to reader benefits (*You can use our standardized tests to free you from time-consuming employment screening*). You'll learn more about special techniques for developing sales and persuasive messages in Chapter 7.

Closing Pleasantly

To avoid abruptness, include a pleasant closing remark that shows your willingness to help the reader. Provide extra information if appropriate. Tailor your remarks to fit this letter and this reader. Refer to the information provided or to its use (*The enclosed list summarizes our recommendations. We wish you all the best in redesigning your Web site*). Since everyone appreciates being recognized as an individual, avoid form-letter closings such as *If we may be of further assistance, ...*

FIGURE 6.3   • **Direct Reply Letter**

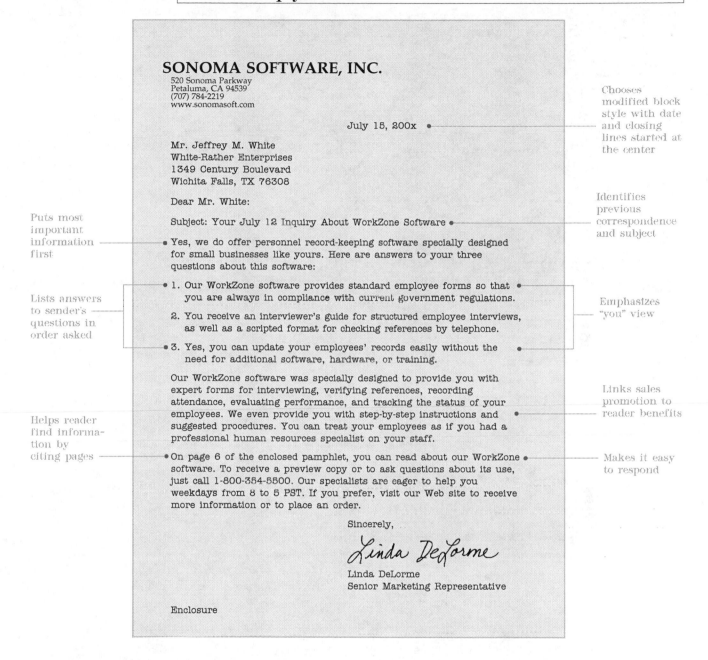

Chooses
modified block
style with date
and closing
lines started at
the center

Puts most
important
information
first

Lists answers
to sender's
questions in
order asked

Helps reader
find informa-
tion by
citing pages

Identifies
previous
correspondence
and subject

Emphasizes
"you" view

Links sales
promotion to
reader benefits

Makes it easy
to respond

SONOMA SOFTWARE, INC.
520 Sonoma Parkway
Petaluma, CA 94539
(707) 784-2219
www.sonomasoft.com

July 15, 200x

Mr. Jeffrey M. White
White-Rather Enterprises
1349 Century Boulevard
Wichita Falls, TX 76308

Dear Mr. White:

Subject: Your July 12 Inquiry About WorkZone Software

Yes, we do offer personnel record-keeping software specially designed for small businesses like yours. Here are answers to your three questions about this software:

1. Our WorkZone software provides standard employee forms so that you are always in compliance with current government regulations.

2. You receive an interviewer's guide for structured employee interviews, as well as a scripted format for checking references by telephone.

3. Yes, you can update your employees' records easily without the need for additional software, hardware, or training.

Our WorkZone software was specially designed to provide you with expert forms for interviewing, verifying references, recording attendance, evaluating performance, and tracking the status of your employees. We even provide you with step-by-step instructions and suggested procedures. You can treat your employees as if you had a professional human resources specialist on your staff.

On page 6 of the enclosed pamphlet, you can read about our WorkZone software. To receive a preview copy or to ask questions about its use, just call 1-800-354-5500. Our specialists are eager to help you weekdays from 8 to 5 PST. If you prefer, visit our Web site to receive more information or to place an order.

Sincerely,

Linda DeLorme

Linda DeLorme
Senior Marketing Representative

Enclosure

ADJUSTMENT LETTERS

When a company responds favorably to a customer's claim, the response is called an adjustment.

Even the best-run and best-loved businesses occasionally receive claims or complaints from consumers. When a company receives a claim and decides to respond favorably, the letter is called an *adjustment letter*. Most businesses make adjustments promptly—they replace merchandise, refund money, extend discounts, send coupons, and repair goods. Businesses make favorable adjustments to legitimate claims for two reasons. First, consumers are protected by contractual and tort law for recovery of damages. If, for example, you find an insect in a package of frozen peas, the food processor of that package is bound by contractual law to replace it. If you suffer injury, the processor may be liable for damages. Second, and more obviously, most organizations genuinely want to satisfy their customers and retain their business.

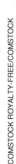

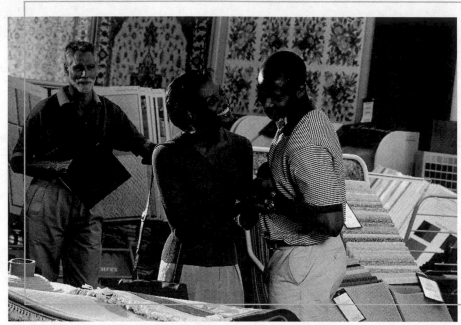

Whether selling carpets, computers, or cars, businesses want happy customers. When something goes wrong, most companies try their best to satisfy their customers. Research shows that seven out of ten customers who complain will do business with the company again so long as their concern is handled properly. Adjustment letters respond to customer complaints.

To compete globally and to pump up local markets, most businesses recognize the value of retaining current customers. A survey of financial services companies revealed that the average cost to retain a customer was $57. To recruit a new customer cost a whopping $279. One way to retain customers is to listen to what they have to say—even when it's a complaint. For many reasons, businesses are eager to respond to customer claims and retain the customer's goodwill.

In responding to customer claims, you must first decide whether to grant the claim. Unless the claim is obviously fraudulent or represents an excessive sum, you'll probably grant it. When you say *yes*, your adjustment letter will be good news to the reader, so you'll want to use the direct pattern. When your response is *no*, the indirect pattern might be more appropriate. Chapter 8 discusses the indirect pattern for conveying negative news.

> **Favorable responses to customer claims follow the direct pattern; unfavorable responses follow the indirect pattern.**

In responding to a claim, you have three goals:

- To rectify the wrong, if one exists
- To regain the confidence of the customer
- To promote future business and goodwill

In responding favorably to a claim, use the direct strategy described in the following writing plan:

Writing Plan for Adjustment Letters

- *Subject line:* (optional) Identify the previous correspondence and make a general reference to the main topic.
- *Opening:* Grant the request or announce the adjustment immediately. Include sales promotion if appropriate.
- *Body:* Provide details about how you are complying with the request. Try to regain the customer's confidence; include sales promotion if appropriate.
- *Closing:* End positively with a forward-looking thought; express confidence in future business relations. Avoid referring to unpleasantness.

Revealing Good News in the Opening

Readers want to learn the good news immediately.

Instead of beginning with a review of what went wrong, present the good news immediately. When Amy Hopkins responded to the claim of customer Sound Systems, Inc., about a missing shipment, her first draft, shown at the top of Figure 6.4, was angry. No wonder. Sound Systems had apparently provided the wrong shipping address, and the goods were returned. But once Amy and her company decided to send a second shipment and comply with the customer's claim, she had to give up the anger and strive to retain the goodwill and the business of this customer. The improved version of her letter announces that a new shipment will arrive shortly.

© Ted Goff (www.tedgoff.com)

If you decide to comply with a customer's claim, let the receiver know immediately. Don't begin your letter with a negative statement (*We are very sorry to hear that you are having trouble with your dishwasher*). This approach reminds the reader of the problem and may rekindle the heated emotions or unhappy feelings experienced when the claim was written. Instead, focus on the good news. The following openings for various letters illustrate how to begin a message with good news:

> You're right! We agree that the warranty on your American Standard Model UC600 dishwasher should be extended for six months.

> You will be receiving shortly a new slim Nokia 8860 cell phone to replace the one that shattered when dropped recently.

> Please take your portable Admiral microwave oven to A-1 Appliance Service, 200 Orange Street, Pasadena, where it will be repaired at no cost to you.

> The enclosed check for $325 demonstrates our desire to satisfy our customers and earn their confidence.

Be enthusiastic, not grudging, when making an adjustment.

In announcing that you will make an adjustment, be sure to do so without a grudging tone—even if you have reservations about whether the claim is legitimate. Once you decide to comply with the customer's request, do so happily. Avoid halfhearted or reluctant responses (*Although the American Standard dishwasher works well when used properly, we have decided to allow you to take yours to A-1 Appliance Service for repair at our expense*).

CATHY

Cathy © Cathy Guisewite. Reprinted with permission of Universal Press Syndicate. All rights reserved.

FIGURE 6.4 ┤ • **Customer Adjustment Letter** ├

before revision

Fails to reveal good
news immediately and
blames customer

Creates ugly tone with
negative words and
sarcasm

Sounds grudging and
reluctant in granting
claim

Gentlemen:

In response to your recent complaint about a missing shipment, it's very difficult to deliver merchandise when we have been given an erroneous address.

Our investigators looked into your problem shipment and determined that it was sent immediately after we received the order. According to the shipper's records, it was delivered to the warehouse address given on your stationery: 3590 University Avenue, St. Paul, Minnesota 55114. Unfortunately, no one at that address would accept delivery, so the shipment was returned to us. I see from your current stationery that your company has a new address. With the proper address, we probably could have delivered this shipment.

Although we feel that it is entirely appropriate to charge you shipping and restocking fees, as is our standard practice on returned goods, in this instance we will waive those fees. We hope this second shipment finally catches up with you at your current address.

Sincerely,

Amy Hopkins

after revision

Ew **ELECTRONIC WAREHOUSE**

930 Abbott Park Place   Phone: (401) 876-8201
Providence, RI 02903-5309   Fax: (401) 876-8345
                                         Web: www.ewarehouse.com

February 21, 200x

Mr. Jeremy Garber
Sound Systems, Inc.
2293 Second Avenue
St. Paul, MN 55120

Dear Mr. Garber: •

Subject: Your February 14 Letter About Your Purchase Order

You should receive by February 25 a second shipment of the speakers, DVDs, • headphones, and other electronic equipment that you ordered January 20.

The first shipment of this order was delivered January 28 to 3590 University Avenue, St. Paul, Minnesota 55114. When no one at that address would accept the shipment, it was returned to us. Now that I have your letter, I see that the order should have been sent to 2293 Second Avenue, St. Paul, Minnesota 55120. When an order is undeliverable, we usually try to verify the shipping address • by telephoning the customer. Somehow the return of this shipment was not caught by our normally painstaking shipping clerks. You can be sure that I will investigate shipping and return procedures with our clerks immediately to see whether we can improve existing methods.

Your respect is important to us, Mr. Garber. Although our rock-bottom discount prices have enabled us to build a volume business, we don't want to be so large that we lose touch with valued customers like you. Over the years • our customers' respect has made us successful, and we hope that the prompt delivery of this shipment will retain yours.

Sincerely,

Amy Hopkins

Amy Hopkins
Distribution Manager

c: David Cole
   Shipping Department

Uses customer's name
in salutation

Announces good news
immediately

Regains confidence of
customer by
explaining what
happened and by
suggesting plans for
improvement

Closes confidently
with genuine appeal
for customer's respect

Explaining Compliance in the Body

Most businesses comply with claims because they want to promote customer goodwill.

In responding to claims, most organizations sincerely want to correct a wrong. They want to do more than just make the customer happy. They want to stand behind their products and services; they want to do what's right.

In the body of the letter, explain how you are complying with the claim. In all but the most routine claims, you should also seek to regain the confidence of the customer. You might reasonably expect that a customer who has experienced difficulty with a product, with delivery, with billing, or with service has lost faith in your organization. Rebuilding that faith is important for future business.

How to rebuild lost confidence depends on the situation and the claim. If procedures need to be revised, explain what changes will be made. If a product has defective parts, tell how the product is being improved. If service is faulty, describe genuine efforts to improve it. Notice in Figure 6.4 that the writer promises to investigate shipping procedures to see whether improvements might prevent future mishaps.

Sometimes the problem is not with the product but with the way it's being used. In other instances customers misunderstand warranties or inadvertently cause delivery and billing mix-ups by supplying incorrect information. Remember that rational and sincere explanations will do much to regain the confidence of unhappy customers.

Because negative words suggest blame and fault, avoid them in letters that attempt to build customer goodwill.

In your explanation avoid emphasizing negative words such as *trouble, regret, misunderstanding, fault, defective, error, inconvenience,* and *unfortunately.* Keep your message positive and upbeat.

Deciding Whether to Apologize

Whether to apologize is a debatable issue. Studies of adjustment letters received by consumers show that a majority do contain apologies, either in the opening or in the closing.[2] Attorneys generally discourage apologies fearing that they admit responsibility and will trigger lawsuits. But an analysis of case outcomes indicates that both judges and juries tend to look on apologies favorably. A few states are even passing laws that protect those who apologize.[3] Some business writing experts advise against apologies, contending that they are counterproductive and merely remind the customer of unpleasantness related to the claim. If, however, it seems natural to you to apologize, do so. People like to hear apologies. It raises their self-esteem, shows the humility of the writer, and acts as a form of "psychological compensation."[4] Don't, however, fall back on the familiar phrase, *I'm sorry for any inconvenience we may have caused.* It sounds mechanical and insincere. Instead, try something like this: *We understand the frustration our delay has caused you, We're sorry you didn't receive better service,* or *You're right to be disappointed.* If you feel that an apology is appropriate, do it early and briefly. Remember, however, that the primary focus of your letter is on (1) how you are complying with the request, (2) how the problem occurred, and (3) how you are working to prevent its recurrence.

Apologize if it seems natural and appropriate.

Using Sensitive Language

The language of adjustment letters must be particularly sensitive, since customers are already upset. Here are some don'ts:

- Don't use negative words (*trouble, regret, misunderstanding, fault, error, inconvenience, you claim*).
- Don't blame customers—even when they may be at fault.
- Don't blame individuals or departments within your organization; it's unprofessional.
- Don't make unrealistic promises; you can't guarantee that the situation will never recur.

Avoiding negative language retains customer goodwill, and resale information rebuilds customer confidence.

To regain the confidence of your reader, consider including resale information. Describe a product's features and any special applications that might appeal to the reader. Promote a new product if it seems appropriate.

Showing Confidence in the Closing

Close an adjustment letter with appreciation, thanks for past business, a desire to be of service, or the promotion of a new product.

End positively by expressing confidence that the problem has been resolved and that continued business relations will result. You might mention the product in a favorable light, suggest a new product, express your appreciation for the customer's business, or anticipate future business. It's often appropriate to refer to the desire to be of service and to satisfy customers. Notice how the following closings illustrate a positive, confident tone:

> You were most helpful in informing us of this situation and permitting us to correct it. We appreciate your thoughtfulness in writing to us.

> Thanks for writing. Your satisfaction is important to us. We hope that this refund check convinces you that service to our customers is our No. 1 priority. Our goals are to earn your confidence and continue to justify that confidence with quality products and excellent service.

> Your flat panel Inspiron 1200 Notebook will come in handy whether you're working at home or on the road. And you can upgrade to a 17-inch display for only $100. Take a look at the enclosed booklet detailing the big savings for essential technology on a budget. We value your business and look forward to your future orders.

LETTERS OF RECOMMENDATION

Letters of recommendation present honest, objective evaluations of individuals and help match candidates to jobs.

Letters of recommendation may be written to nominate people for awards and for membership in organizations. More frequently, though, they are written to evaluate present or former employees. The central concern in these messages is honesty. Thus, you should avoid exaggerating or distorting a candidate's qualifications to cover up weaknesses or to destroy the person's chances. Ethically and legally, you have a duty to the candidate as well as to other employers to describe that person truthfully and objectively. You don't, however, have to endorse everyone who asks. Since recommendations are generally voluntary, you can—and should—resist writing letters for individuals you can't truthfully support. Ask these people to find other recommenders who know them better.

Some businesspeople today refuse to write recommendations for former employees because they fear lawsuits. Other businesspeople argue that recommendations are useless because they're always positive. Despite the general avoidance of

Letters of recommendation make a big difference to employment candidates. Well-written letters help match candidates with jobs. To be safe, writers should focus on information necessary to evaluate job performance.

negatives, well-written recommendations do help match candidates with jobs. Hiring companies learn more about a candidate's skills and potential. As a result, they are able to place a candidate properly. Therefore, you should learn to write such letters because you will surely be expected to do so in your future career.

For letters of recommendation, use the direct strategy as described in the following writing plan:

Writing Plan for a Letter of Recommendation

- *Opening:* Identify the applicant, the position, and the reason for writing. State that the message is confidential. Establish your relationship with the applicant. Describe the length of employment or relationship.
- *Body:* Describe job duties. Provide specific examples of the applicant's professional and personal skills and attributes. Compare the applicant with others in his or her field.
- *Closing:* Summarize the significant attributes of the applicant. Offer an overall rating. Draw a conclusion regarding the recommendation.

Identifying the Purpose in the Opening

The opening names the candidate, identifies the purpose, and describes the relationship of the writer.

Begin an employment recommendation by identifying the candidate and the position sought, if you know it. State that your remarks are confidential, and suggest that you are writing at the request of the applicant. Describe your relationship with the candidate, as shown in the first paragraph of the employment recommendation letter in Figure 6.5. Letters that recommend individuals for awards may open with more supportive statements, such as, *I'm very pleased to nominate Robert Walsh for the Employee-of-the-Month award. For the past 16 months, Mr. Walsh served as staff accountant in my division. During that time he distinguished himself by . . . .*

Providing Evidence in the Body

The body of an employment recommendation should describe the candidate's job performance and potential in specific terms.

The body of an employment recommendation should describe the applicant's job performance and potential. Employers are particularly interested in such traits as communication skills, organizational skills, people skills, the ability to work with a team, the ability to work independently, honesty, dependability, ambition, loyalty, and initiative. In describing these traits, be sure to back them up with evidence. One of the biggest weaknesses in letters of recommendation is that writers tend to make global, nonspecific statements (*He was careful and accurate* versus *He completed eight financial statements monthly with about 99 percent accuracy*). Employers prefer definite, task-related descriptions, as shown in the second and third paragraphs of Figure 6.5.

Be especially careful to support any negative comments with verification (not *He was slower than other customer service reps* but *He answered 18 calls an hour, whereas most service reps average 30 calls an hour*). In reporting deficiencies, be sure to describe behavior (*her last two reports were late and had to be rewritten by her supervisor*) rather than evaluate it (*she is unreliable and her reports are careless*).

Evaluating in the Closing

The closing presents an overall evaluation and may encourage a telephone call.

In the final paragraph of a recommendation, you should offer an overall evaluation. Indicate how you would rank this person in relation to others in similar positions. Many managers add a statement indicating whether they would rehire the applicant, given the chance. If you are strongly supportive, summarize the candidate's best qualities. In the closing you might also offer to answer questions by telephone. Such a statement, though, could suggest that the candidate has weak skills and that you will make damaging statements orally but not in print.

General letters of recommendation, written when the candidate has no specific position in mind, often begin with the salutation TO PROSPECTIVE EMPLOYERS. More

FIGURE 6.5   • **Employment Recommendation Letter**

ST. ELIZABETH'S HOSPITAL

2404 Euclid Avenue
Cleveland, OH 44414-2900
216-439-8700
ww.stelizabeth.com

February 21, 200x

Vice President, Human Resources
Healthcare Enterprises
3529 Springfield Street
Cincinnati, OH 45890

Illustrates simplified letter style — • RECOMMENDATION OF LANCE W. OLIVER

Identifies applicant and position — • At the request of Lance W. Oliver, I submit this confidential information in • *Mentions confidentiality of message*
support of his application for the position of assistant director in your Human
Resources Department. Mr. Oliver served under my supervision as assistant • *Tells relationship to writer*
director of Guest Relations at St. Elizabeth's Hospital for the past three years. •

Supports general qualities with specific details — • Mr. Oliver was in charge of many customer service programs for our 770-bed
hospital. A large part of his job involved monitoring and improving patient
satisfaction. Because of his personable nature and superior people skills, he got
along well with fellow employees, patients, and physicians. His personnel record
includes a number of "Gotcha" citations, given to employees caught in the act of
performing exemplary service.

• Mr. Oliver works well with a team, as evidenced by his participation on the
steering committee to develop our "Service First Every Day" program. His most
significant contributions to our hospital, though, came as a result of his own *Describes and interprets accomplishments*
creativity and initiative. He developed and implemented a patient hotline to
hear complaints and resolve problems immediately. This enormously successful •
telephone service helped us improve our patient satisfaction rating from 7.2
last year to 8.4 this year. That's the highest rating in our history, and
Mr. Oliver deserves a great deal of the credit.

Summarizes main points and offers evaluation — • We're sorry to lose Mr. Oliver, but we recognize his desire to advance his
career. I am confident that his resourcefulness, intelligence, and enthusiasm
will make him successful in your organization. I recommend him without
reservation.

Mary E. O'Rourke

MARY E. O'ROURKE, DIRECTOR, GUEST RELATIONS

MEO:rtd

Tips for Writing Letters of Recommendation
- Identify the purpose and confidentiality of the message.
- Establish your relationship with the applicant.
- Describe the length of employment and job duties, if relevant.
- Provide specific examples of the applicant's professional and personal skills.
- Compare the applicant with others in the same field.
- Offer an overall rating of the applicant.
- Summarize the significant attributes of the applicant.
- Draw a conclusion regarding the recommendation.

specific recommendations, to support applications to known positions, address an individual. When the addressee's name is unknown, consider using the simplified letter format, shown in Figure 6.5, which avoids a salutation.

• WRITING WINNING GOODWILL MESSAGES

Written goodwill messages carry more meaning than ready-made cards.

Goodwill messages, which include thanks, recognition, and sympathy, seem to intimidate many communicators. Finding the right words to express feelings is sometimes more difficult than writing ordinary business documents. Writers tend to procrastinate when it comes to goodwill messages, or else they send a ready-made card or pick up the telephone. Remember, though, that the personal sentiments of the sender are always more expressive and more meaningful to readers than are printed cards or oral messages. Taking the time to write gives more importance to our well-wishing. Personal notes also provide a record that can be reread, savored, and treasured.

Messages that express thanks, recognition, and sympathy should be written promptly.

In expressing thanks, recognition, or sympathy, you should always do so promptly. These messages are easier to write when the situation is fresh in your mind. They also mean more to the recipient. What's more, a prompt thank-you note carries the hidden message that you care and that you consider the event to be important. You will learn to write four kinds of goodwill messages—thanks, congratulations, praise, and sympathy. Instead of writing plans for each of them, we recommend that you concentrate on the five Ss. Goodwill messages should be:

- **Selfless.** Be sure to focus the message solely on the receiver, not the sender. Don't talk about yourself; avoid such comments as *I remember when I . . . .*
- **Specific.** Personalize the message by mentioning specific incidents or characteristics of the receiver. Telling a colleague *Great speech* is much less effective than *Great story about McDonald's marketing in Moscow.* Take care to verify names and other facts.
- **Sincere.** Let your words show genuine feelings. Rehearse in your mind how you would express the message to the receiver orally. Then transform that conversational language to your written message. Avoid pretentious, formal, or flowery language (*It gives me great pleasure to extend felicitations on the occasion of your firm's twentieth anniversary*).
- **Spontaneous.** Keep the message fresh and enthusiastic. Avoid canned phrases (*Congratulations on your promotion, Good luck in the future*). Strive for directness and naturalness, not creative brilliance.
- **Short.** Although goodwill messages can be as long as needed, try to accomplish your purpose in only a few sentences. What is most important is remembering an individual. Such caring does not require documentation or wordiness. Individuals and business organizations often use special note cards or stationery for brief messages.

Thanks

When someone has done you a favor or when an action merits praise, you need to extend thanks or show appreciation. Letters of appreciation may be written to customers for their orders, to hosts and hostesses for their hospitality, to individuals for kindnesses performed, and especially to customers who complain. After all, complainers are actually providing you with free consulting reports from the field. Complainers who feel that they were listened to often become the greatest promoters of an organization.[5]

Send letters of thanks to customers, hosts, and individuals who have performed kind acts.

Because the receiver will be pleased to hear from you, you can open directly with the purpose of your message. The letter in Figure 6.6 thanks a speaker who addressed a group of marketing professionals. Although such thank-you notes can be quite short, this one is a little longer because the writer wants to lend importance to the receiver's efforts. Notice that every sentence relates to the receiver and offers

FIGURE 6.6 • **Favor Thank-you**

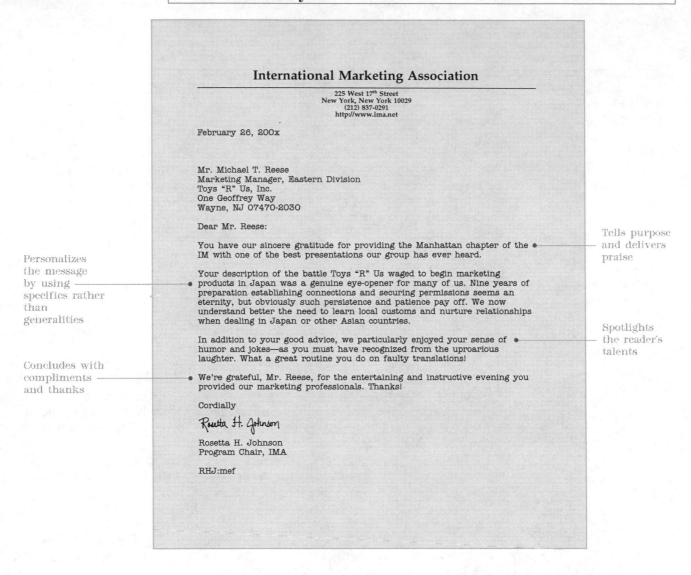

International Marketing Association

225 West 17th Street
New York, New York 10029
(212) 837-0291
http://www.ima.net

February 26, 200x

Mr. Michael T. Reese
Marketing Manager, Eastern Division
Toys "R" Us, Inc.
One Geoffrey Way
Wayne, NJ 07470-2030

Dear Mr. Reese:

You have our sincere gratitude for providing the Manhattan chapter of the
IM with one of the best presentations our group has ever heard.

Your description of the battle Toys "R" Us waged to begin marketing
products in Japan was a genuine eye-opener for many of us. Nine years of
preparation establishing connections and securing permissions seems an
eternity, but obviously such persistence and patience pay off. We now
understand better the need to learn local customs and nurture relationships
when dealing in Japan or other Asian countries.

In addition to your good advice, we particularly enjoyed your sense of
humor and jokes—as you must have recognized from the uproarious
laughter. What a great routine you do on faulty translations!

We're grateful, Mr. Reese, for the entertaining and instructive evening you
provided our marketing professionals. Thanks!

Cordially

Rosetta H. Johnson

Rosetta H. Johnson
Program Chair, IMA

RHJ:mef

Margin annotations:

Tells purpose and delivers praise

Personalizes the message by using specifics rather than generalities

Spotlights the reader's talents

Concludes with compliments and thanks

---

enthusiastic praise. By using the receiver's name along with contractions and positive words, the writer makes the letter sound warm and conversational.

Should you use e-mail or e-cards to send goodwill messages? Although electronic messages may be acceptable for close friends or in isolated instances, goodwill messages sent by land mail are much better. Recently an employee wrote to etiquette maven Miss Manners. He said that he had been invited to the home of his boss for a formal dinner. He thanked his boss by sending him an e-card. Later he noticed that his boss seemed remote. Miss Manners asked whether the boss had served him dinner out of a can. If not, then why send him a canned thank-you?

Personally written notes that show appreciation and express thanks are significant to their receivers. In expressing thanks, you generally write a short note on special notepaper or heavy card stock. It's acceptable to print the message on a computer, perhaps in a script font, but use special paper. The following messages provide models for expressing thanks for a gift, for a favor, and for hospitality.

E-mail and e-cards are inappropriate for serious thank-you and other goodwill messages.

To Express Thanks for a Gift

Identify the gift, tell why you appreciate it, and explain how you will use it.

Thanks, Laura, to you and the other members of the department for honoring me with the elegant Waterford crystal vase at the party celebrating my twentieth anniversary with the company.

The height and shape of the vase are perfect to hold roses and other bouquets from my garden. Each time I fill it, I'll remember your thoughtfulness in choosing this lovely gift for me.

To Send Thanks for a Favor

Tell what the favor means using sincere, simple statements.

I sincerely appreciate your filling in for me last week when I was too ill to attend the planning committee meeting for the spring exhibition.

Without your participation much of my preparatory work would have been lost. It's comforting to know that competent and generous individuals like you are part of our team, Mark. Moreover, it's my very good fortune to be able to count you as a friend. I'm grateful to you.

To Extend Thanks for Hospitality

Compliment the fine food, charming surroundings, warm hospitality, excellent host and hostess, and good company.

Jeffrey and I want you to know how much we enjoyed the dinner party for our department that you hosted Saturday evening. Your charming home and warm hospitality, along with the lovely dinner and sinfully delicious chocolate dessert, combined to create a truly memorable evening.

Most of all, though, we appreciate your kindness in cultivating togetherness in our department. Thanks, Jennifer, for being such a special person.

Goodwill Response

Take the time to respond to any goodwill message you may receive.

Should you respond when you receive a congratulatory note or a written pat on the back? By all means! These messages are attempts to connect personally; they are efforts to reach out, to form professional and/or personal bonds. Failing to respond to notes of congratulations and most other goodwill messages is like failing to say "You're welcome" when someone says "Thank you." Responding to such messages is simply the right thing to do. Do avoid, though, minimizing your achievements with comments that suggest that you don't really deserve the praise or that the sender is exaggerating your good qualities.

To Answer a Congratulatory Note

Thanks for your kind words regarding my award, and thanks, too, for sending me the newspaper clipping. I truly appreciate your thoughtfulness and warm wishes.

To Respond to a Pat on the Back

Your note about my work made me feel good. I'm grateful for your thoughtfulness.

Sympathy

Sympathy notes should refer to the misfortune sensitively and offer assistance.

Most of us can bear misfortune and grief more easily when we know that others care. Notes expressing sympathy, though, are probably more difficult to write than any other kind of message. Commercial "In sympathy" cards make the task easier—but they are far less meaningful. Grieving friends want to know what you think—not what Hallmark's card writers think. To help you get started, you can always glance through cards expressing sympathy. They will supply ideas about the kinds of thoughts you might wish to convey in your own words. In writing a sympathy note, (1) refer to the death or misfortune sensitively, using words that show you understand what a crushing blow it is; (2) in the case of a death, praise the deceased in a personal way; (3) offer assistance without going into excessive detail; and (4) end on a reassuring, forward-looking note. Sympathy messages may be typed, although handwriting seems more personal. In either case, use notepaper or personal stationery.

In condolence notes mention the loss tactfully and recognize the good qualities of the deceased.

To Express Condolences

We are deeply saddened, Gayle, to learn of the death of your husband. Warren's kind nature and friendly spirit endeared him to all who knew him. He will be missed.

Assure the receiver of your concern. Offer assistance.

Although words seem empty in expressing our grief, we want you to know that your friends at QuadCom extend their profound sympathy to you. If we may help you or lighten your load in any way, you have but to call.

Conclude on a positive, reassuring note.

We know that the treasured memories of your many happy years together, along with the support of your family and many friends, will provide strength and comfort in the months ahead.

SUMMING UP AND LOOKING FORWARD

In this chapter you learned to write letters that request information, make direct claims, respond favorably to information requests, and make adjustments. You also learned to write letters of recommendation and a variety of goodwill messages. All of these everyday business messages use the direct strategy. They open immediately with the main idea followed by details and explanations. Not all messages, however, are straightforward. In the next chapter you'll learn to use the indirect pattern when you must be persuasive.

CRITICAL THINKING

1. A recent article in a professional magazine carried this headline: "Is Letter Writing Dead?"[6] How would you respond to such a question?

2. Which is more effective in claim letters—anger or objectivity? Why?

3. Is it insensitive to include resale or sales promotion information in an adjustment letter?

4. Why is it important to regain the confidence of a customer when you respond to a claim letter?

5. Is it appropriate for businesspeople to write goodwill messages expressing thanks, recognition, and sympathy to business acquaintances? Why or why not?

CHAPTER REVIEW

6. Under what conditions is it important to send business letters rather than e-mail messages?

7. What determines whether you write a letter directly or indirectly?

8. What are the two most important positions in a letter?

9. List two ways that you could begin a direct inquiry letter that asks many questions.

10. What three elements are appropriate in the closing of a request for information?

11. What is a claim letter? Give an original example.

12. What are the three goals of a writer of an adjustment letter?

13. Why do some companies comply with nearly all claims?

14. What information should the opening in a letter of recommendation include?

15. The best goodwill messages include what five characteristics?

WRITING IMPROVEMENT EXERCISES

Letter-Opening Choices
Your Task. Indicate which of the following entries represents an effective direct opening.

16. a. Will you please allow me to introduce myself. I am Daryl Davidson, and I am assistant to the director of Human Resources at MicroSynergy. Our company has an intranet, which we would like to use more efficiently to elicit feedback on employee issues and concerns. I understand that you have a software product called "Opinionware" that might do this, and I need to ask you some questions about it.
    b. Please answer the following questions about your software product "Opinionware," which we are considering for our intranet.

17. a. Thank you for your e-mail of March 22 in which you inquired about the availability of a CD burner and DVD combo drive.
    b. We have on hand an ample supply of CD burner/DVD combo drives.

18. a. Yes, the next Michigan Computer Show featuring the latest computer hardware and software will be held in the Gibraltar Trade Center from April 15–18.
    b. This will acknowledge receipt of your inquiry of December 2 in which you ask about the next Michigan Computer Show.

19. a. Your letter of July 26 requesting a refund has been referred to me because Mr. Avila is away   _____
       from the office.
    b. Your refund check for $175 is enclosed.

Direct Openings

Your Task. Revise the following openings so that they are more direct. Add information if necessary.

20. My name is Brandon Brockway, and I am assistant to the manager of Information Services & Technology at HealthCentral, Inc. Our company needs to do a better job of integrating human resources and payroll functions. I understand that you have a software product called "HRFocus" that might do this, and I need to ask you some questions about it.

21. Anderson Associates has undertaken a management initiative to pursue an internship program. I have been appointed as the liaison person to conduct research regarding our proposed program. We are fully aware of the benefits of a strong internship program, and our management team is eager to take advantage of some of these benefits. We would be deeply appreciative if you would be kind enough to help me out with answers to a number of specific questions.

22. Your letter of March 4 has been referred to me. Pursuant to your inquiry, I have researched your question in regard to whether or not we offer our European-style patio umbrella in colors. This unique umbrella is one of our most popular items. Its 10-foot canopy protects you when the sun is directly overhead, but it also swivels and tilts to virtually any angle for continuous sun protection all day long. It comes in two colors: cream and forest green.

23. Pursuant to your inquiry of June 14, which was originally sent to *Classic Motorcycle Magazine*, I am happy to respond to you. In your letter you ask about the tire choices for the Superbike and Superstock teams competing at the Honda Superbike Classic in Alabama. As you noted, the track temperatures reached above 125 degrees and the new asphalt surface had an abrasive effect on tires. With the added heat and reduced grip, nearly all of the riders in the competition selected Dunlop Blue Groove hard compound front and rear tires.

24. I am pleased to receive your inquiry regarding the possibility of my acting as a speaker at the final semester meeting of your business management club meeting on May 2. The topic of online résumés interests me and is one on which I think I could impart helpful information to your members. Therefore, I am responding in the affirmative to your kind invitation.

25. Thank you for your recent order of February 4. We are sure your customers and employees will love the high-quality Color-Block Sweatshirts with an 80/20 cotton/polyester blend that you ordered from our spring catalog. Your order is currently being processed and should leave our warehouse in Iowa in mid-February. We use UPS for all deliveries in southern California. Because you ordered sweatshirts with your logo embroidered in a two-tone combination, your order cannot be shipped until February 18. You should not expect it until about February 20.

26. We have just received your letter of October 3 regarding the unfortunate troubles you are having with your Premier DVD player. In your letter you ask if you may send the flawed DVD player to us for inspection. It is our normal practice to handle all service requests through our local dealers. However, in your circumstance we are willing to take a look at your unit here at our Columbus plant. Therefore, please send it to us so that we may determine what's wrong.

Closing Paragraph

Your Task. The following concluding paragraph to a claim letter response suffers from faults in strategy, tone, and emphasis. Revise and improve.

27. As a result of your complaint of November 3, we are sending a replacement shipment of PC power packs by BigDog Express. Unfortunately, this shipment will not reach you until November 10. We hope that you will not allow this troubling incident and the resulting inconvenience and lost sales you suffered to jeopardize our future business relations. In the past we have been able to provide you with quality products and prompt service.

WRITING COACH
STEP-BY-STEP DEMONSTRATION

Direct Request Letter

Problem

As the office manager at Earth Systems, you are responsible for equipment. The operations chief, Eric Young, sits down at your desk and says, "Look, we've just received a notice from our insurance carrier telling us that we have to secure our office equipment or else our rates will increase. How many pieces of equipment do we have? Can you get some figures on how much this will cost?" Counting the computers in private offices, you figure that the company has 18 workstations consisting of computers, monitors, and keyboards plus 12 printers. But you are worried about installing security devices that might tie the computers to desktops and make it impossible to move them around. You realize, of course, that office theft can be a problem. After checking local sources for security devices, you decide to write to a national supplier, Micro Supplies and Software, to get an estimate.

before revision

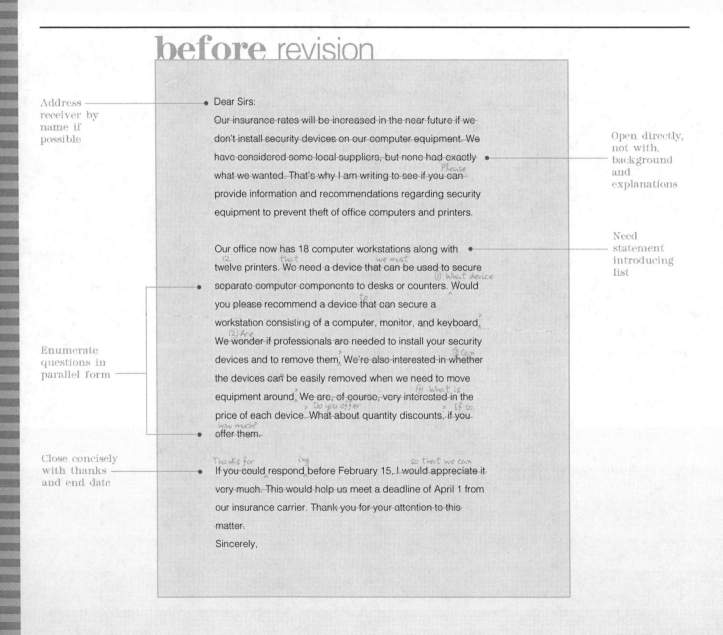

Address receiver by name if possible

Dear Sirs:

Our insurance rates will be increased in the near future if we don't install security devices on our computer equipment. We have considered some local suppliers, but none had exactly what we wanted. That's why I am writing to see if you can *Please* provide information and recommendations regarding security equipment to prevent theft of office computers and printers.

Open directly, not with background and explanations

Our office now has 18 computer workstations along with twelve printers. We need a device that can be used to secure separate computer components to desks or counters. Would you please recommend a device that can secure a workstation consisting of a computer, monitor, and keyboard. We wonder if professionals are needed to install your security devices and to remove them. We're also interested in whether the devices can be easily removed when we need to move equipment around. We are, of course, very interested in the price of each device. What about quantity discounts, if you offer them.

Need statement introducing list

Enumerate questions in parallel form

Close concisely with thanks and end date

If you could respond before February 15, I would appreciate it very much. This would help us meet a deadline of April 1 from our insurance carrier. Thank you for your attention to this matter.

Sincerely,

Writing Plan

OPENING

Ask the most important question first or express a polite command.

The purpose of this letter is to request information about security devices. The primary audience will be staff members at a company that wants to sell such devices, so a direct approach is appropriate.

BODY

Explain the request logically and courteously. Ask other questions if necessary.

Before writing the letter, you need to inventory the current equipment and decide what questions to ask. The questions should be organized into a logical sequence.

CLOSING

Request a specific action with an end date, if appropriate, and show appreciation.

Decide how soon the information is needed to meet the insurance deadline.

---

after revision

EARTII SYSTEMS

| Geotechnical Engineers | www.earthsystems.com | (805) 558-8791 |
| 4439 Hitchcock Way | Ventura, CA 93105 | |

January 28, 200x

Mr. Jeff Lee, Customer Service
Micro Supplies and Software
P.O. Box 6418
Fort Atkinson, WI 53538

Dear Mr. Lee:

Please provide information and recommendations regarding security equipment to prevent theft of office computers and printers.

Our office now has 18 computer workstations and 12 printers that we must secure to desks or counters. Answers to the following questions will help us select the best devices for our purposes:

1. What device would you recommend to secure a workstation consisting of a computer, monitor, and keyboard?

2. Are professionals needed to install your security devices and remove them?

3. Can the devices be easily removed when we need to move equipment around?

4. What is the price of each device? Do you offer quantity discounts? If so, how much?

Thanks for responding before February 15 so that we can meet an April 1 deadline from our insurance carrier.

Sincerely,

Deanna Gomez

Deanna Gomez
Office Manager

WRITING IMPROVEMENT CASES

6.1 Direct Request: Las Vegas Conference

The following letter from Brianna Phelps inquires about conference facilities in Las Vegas. Her first draft must be revised.

Your Task. Analyze Brianna's letter. It suffers from many writing faults that you have studied. List its weaknesses and then outline an appropriate writing plan. If your instructor directs, revise the letter.

Current date

Meeting Manager
The Venetian
3355 Las Vegas Boulevard
Las Vegas, NV 89109

Dear Sir:

My name is Brianna Phelps, and I am a recently hired member of the Marketing and Special Events Division of my company, Cynergy. I have been given the assignment of making initial inquiries for the purpose of arranging our next marketing meeting. Pursuant to this assignment, I am writing to you. We would like to find a resort hotel with conference facilities, and we have heard excellent things about The Venetian.

Our marketing meeting will require banquet facilities where we can all be together, but we will also need at least four meeting rooms that are small in size. Each of these rooms should accommodate in the neighborhood of 75. We hope to arrange our conference October 23–27, and we expect about 250 sales associates. Most of our associates will be flying in, so I'm interested in transportation to and from the airport.

Does The Venetian have public address systems in the meeting rooms? Due to the fact that we will be making electronic presentations, how about audio-visual equipment and computer facilities for presentations? I am also interested in learning whether the Sands Convention Center is part of The Venetian. Thank you for your cooperation.

Sincerely,

1. List at least five specific weaknesses in Brianna's letter.

2. Outline a writing plan for an information request.
    Opening:
    Body:
    Closing:

6.2 Direct Reply: McDonald's Goes Green

Fast-food giant McDonald's is often accused of generating excessive litter and abusing the environment with its packaging and products. It receives letters from consumers asking what it is doing to reduce waste and improve the environment.

Your Task. As part of a group of interns at McDonald's, you are to revise the following rough draft of an information response letter to be sent to people inquiring about the company's environmental policies and practices. Analyze the letter and list at least five weaknesses. What writing plan should this letter follow? If your instructor agrees, revise it. Add an appropriate subject line and any additional information you know about McDonald's environmental practices.

Current date

Ms. Julie Kahn
176 Prospect Avenue
Elmhurst, IL 60126

Dear Ms. Kahn:

This is in response to your inquiry about McDonald's environmental policies. As a leader in the fast-food industry, reducing waste and conserving the environment are extremely important to those of us here at McDonald's. Since it began working with the Environmental Defense Fund 80 percent of its restaurant waste stream has been eliminated by McDonald's. McDonald's is reducing it's impact on landfills and world resources. McDonald's have introduced a number of practices that are environmentally-friendly.

For one thing, we are developing new packaging. In fact, we have reduced our polystyrene use by 90 percent. Another thing we are doing is increasing recycling. Our suppliers are using corrugated boxes with at least 35 percent recycled content. Reusable salad lids and shipping pallets, bulk condiment dispensers, and refillable coffee mugs are being tested. Another thing we are doing has to do with composting. More of our restaurants are experimenting with compositing egg shells, coffee grounds, and food scraps. Another thing we are doing has to do with reduced waste. All of our suppliers must meet new waste-reduction goals. And restaurant crews have been retrained to give waste reduction equal priority with quality quickness and cleanliness.

As you can see, McDonald's cares about preserving the earths resources for today. And for the future. We think we are doing a great job in our commitment to conservation. But you can see for yourself by visiting your local McDonald's We hope you will use the enclosed sandwich coupons and experience first hand the changes we're making at McDonald's.

Sincerely,

1.   List at least five weaknesses in the preceding letter.

2.   Outline a writing plan for an information response.
     Subject line:
     Opening:
     Body:

     Closing:

6.3 Claim Letter: Disturbed by Rental Car Charges

Your Task. Analyze the following poorly written letter. List its weaknesses, and outline a writing plan. If your instructor directs, revise the letter.

Current date

Mr. Sergio Harris, Manager
Customer Service
Avon Car Rentals
6501 King Lawrence Road
Raleigh, NC 27607

Dear Customer Service Manager Sergio Harris,

This is to inform you that you can't have it both ways. Either you provide customers with cars with full gas tanks or you don't. And if you don't, you shouldn't charge them when they return with empty tanks!

In view of the fact that I picked up a car in Raleigh August 22 with an empty tank, I had to fill it immediately. Then I drove it until August 25. When I returned to Charlotte, I naturally let the tank go nearly empty, since that is the way I received the car in Raleigh.

But your attendant in Charlotte charged me to fill the tank—$46.50 (premium gasoline at premium prices)! Although I explained to him that I had received it with an empty tank, he kept telling me that company policy required that he charge for a fill-up. My total bill came to $466.50, which, you must agree, is a lot of money for a rental period of only three days. I have the signed rental agreement and a receipt showing that I paid the full amount and that it included $46.50 for a gas fill-up when I returned the car.

Inasmuch as my company is a new customer and inasmuch as we had hoped to use your agency for our future car rentals because of your competitive rates, I trust that you will give this matter your prompt attention.

Disappointedly yours,

1.   List at least five weaknesses.

2.   Outline a writing plan for a claim.
     Opening:
     Body:

     Closing:

ACTIVITIES AND CASES

6.4 Direct Request: Conference at the Fabulous Paris Las Vegas

Your company, Vortex Enterprises, has just had an enormously successful two-year sales period. CEO Kenneth Richardson has asked you, as marketing manager, to arrange a fabulous conference/retreat. "This will be a giant thank-you gift for all 75 of our engineers, product managers, and salespeople," he says. Warming up to the idea, he says, "I want the company to host a four-day combination sales conference/vacation/ retreat at some spectacular location. Let's begin by inquiring at Paris Las Vegas. I hear it's awesome!" You check its Web site and find some general information. However, you decide to write a letter so that you can have a permanent, formal record of all the resorts you investigate. You estimate that your company will require about 75 rooms—preferably with a view of the Strip. You'll also need about three conference rooms for one and a half days. You want to know room rates, conference facilities, and entertainment possibilities for families. The CEO gave you two possible times: July 8–12 or August 18–22. You know that these are off-peak times, and you wonder whether you can get a good room rate. What entertainment will be showing at Paris Las Vegas during these times? One evening the CEO will want to host a banquet for about 140 people. Oh yes, he wants a report from you by March 1.

Your Task: Write a well-organized information request to Ms. Nancy Mercado, Manager, Convention Services, Paris Las Vegas, 281 Paris Drive, Las Vegas, NV 87551. Spell out your needs and conclude with a logical end date.

6.5 Direct Request: Informational Interview

You want to learn more about careers in your field, and you've found someone who is willing to talk to you. The manager you selected is a busy person, and he will try to work a personal interview into his schedule. However, in case he can't meet you in person, he would like to have your questions in letter form so that he could answer them in a telephone conversation if necessary.

Your Task. Write an information request to a real or hypothetical person in a company where you would like to work. If you want to start your own business, write to someone who has done it. Assume that the person has agreed to talk with you, but you haven't set a date. To learn more about informational interviews and how to write questions, look at the "Checklist for Conducting Informational and Other Interviews." It can be found at **Guffey Xtra!** in the online chapter, "Employment and Other Interviewing." Use your imagination in creating five to eight interview questions. Be sure to show appreciation.

TEAM

6.6 Direct Request: Beach Bike Rentals Seeks Web Exposure

As the successful co-owners of Beach Bike Rentals, you and your partner decide that you need a Web site to attract even more business to your resort location. Primarily you rent bicycles and surreys to tourists visiting hotels along the beach. In addition, you carry tandems, pedal go-carts, mountain bikes, slingshot and chopper trikes, and other unique bikes, as well as inline skates.

Business is good at your sunny beachside location, but a Web site would provide 24-hour information and attract a wider audience. The trouble is that you don't know anything about creating, hosting, or maintaining a Web site. Your partner has heard of a local company called Spiderside Web Production, and you decide to inquire about creating a Web site. You and he prefer to write a letter so that you can work on your questions together and create a unified, orderly presentation.

Your Task. In teams of two or three, prepare an information request with logical questions about designing, hosting, and maintaining a Web site for a small business. You are not expected to create the content of the site. That will come later. Instead you want to ask questions about how a Web site is developed. You know for sure that you want a page that invites resort and hotel operators to feature your fun-filled facilities at their sites, but you don't know how to go about it. Address your letter to Richard Wolziac, Spiderside Web Production, 927 El Fuerte Boulevard, Carlsbad, CA 92008. Be sure to include an end date and a reason.

6.7 Direct Request: Krispy Kreme Bake Sale

You've always loved Krispy Kreme doughnuts, so you were delighted to learn that they are now being sold in a nearby shopping center. You also heard that they can be used in fund-raising events. As chair of the spring fund-raising committee for Noah's Ark Children's Center, you need to find out more about how Krispy Kreme's fund-raising partnership works. Do you hold a traditional bake sale or what? How do you make any money if you sell the doughnuts at their regular retail price? You looked at the company's Web site and got basic information. You're still unclear about how certificates work in fund-raising. And what about Krispy Kreme partnership cards? You left a brief note at the Krispy Kreme Web site, but you didn't get a response. Now you decide to write.

Your Task. Compose a letter asking specific questions about how you can partner with Krispy Kreme in raising funds. Use your return address in a personal business letter style (see Figure 6.2). Send your letter to Customer Relations, Krispy Kreme Doughnut Corporation, P.O. Box 83, Winston-Salem, NC 27103. You need feedback by March 1 if you are to use Krispy Kreme in your spring fund-raising event. How do you want Krispy Kreme to respond?

WEB

6.8 Direct Request: Computer Code of Conduct

As an assistant in the campus computer laboratory, you have been asked by your boss to help write a code of conduct for use of the laboratory facilities. This code will spell out what behavior and activities are allowed in your lab. The first thing you are to do is conduct a search of the Internet to see what other college or university computing labs have written as conduct codes.

Your Task. Using at least two search engines, search the Web employing variations of the keywords "Computer Code of Conduct." Print two or three codes that seem appropriate. Write a letter (or an e-mail message, if your instructor agrees) to the director of an educational computer laboratory asking for further information about its code and its effectiveness. Include at least five significant questions. Attach your printouts to your letter.

6.9 Direct Claim: Headaches From "No Surprise" Offer

As vice president of Breakaway Travel Service, you are angry with Virtuoso Enterprises. Virtuoso is a catalog company that provides imprinted promotional products for companies. Your travel service was looking for something special to offer in promoting its cruise ship travel packages. Virtuoso offered free samples of its promotional merchandise, under its "No Surprise" policy.

You figured, what could you lose? So on February 5 you placed a telephone order for a number of samples. These included an insulated lunch sack, an AM-FM travel radio, a square-ended barrel bag with fanny pack, as well as a deluxe canvas attaché case and two colors of garment-dyed sweatshirts. All items were supposed to be free. You did think it odd that you were asked for your company's MasterCard credit number, but Virtuoso promised to bill you only if you kept the samples.

When the items arrived, you were not pleased, and you returned them all on February 11 (you have a postal receipt showing the return). But your March credit statement showed a charge of $229.13 for the sample items. You called Virtuoso in March and spoke to Rachel, who assured you that a credit would be made on your next statement. However, your April statement showed no credit. You called again and received a similar promise. It's now May and no credit has been made. You decide to write and demand action.

Your Task. Write a claim letter that documents the problem and states the action that you want taken. Add any information you feel is necessary. Address your letter to Ms. Paula Loveday, Customer Services, Virtuoso Enterprises, 420 Ninth Street South, LaCrosse, WI 54602.

6.10 Direct Claim: This Desk Is Going Back

As the founder and president of a successful consulting firm, you decided to splurge and purchase a fine executive desk for your own office. You ordered an expensive desk described as "North American white oak embellished with hand-inlaid walnut cross-banding." Although you would not ordinarily purchase large, expensive items by mail, you were impressed by the description of this desk and by the money-back guarantee promised in the catalog.

When the desk arrived, you knew that you had made a mistake. The wood finish was rough, the grain looked splotchy, and many of the drawers would not pull out easily. The advertisement had promised "full suspension, silent ball-bearing drawer slides."

Your Task. Because you are disappointed with the desk, you decide to send it back, taking advantage of the money-back guarantee. Write a claim letter to Patrick Dwiggens, Operations Manager, Premier Wood Products, P.O. Box 528, High Point, NC 27261, asking for your money back. You're not sure whether the freight charges can be refunded, but it's worth a try. Supply any details needed.

6.11 Direct Claim: Backing Out of Project Management Seminar

Ace Executive Training Institute offered a seminar titled "Enterprise Project Management Protocol" that sounded terrific. It promised to teach project managers how to estimate work, report status, write work packages, and cope with project conflicts. Because your company often is engaged in large cross-functional projects, it decided to send four key managers to the seminar to be held June 1–2 at the Ace headquarters in Pittsburgh. The fee was $2,200 each, and it was paid in advance. About six weeks before the seminar, you learned that three of the managers would be tied up in projects that would not be completed in time for them to attend.

Your Task. On your company letterhead, write a claim letter to Addison O'Neill, Registrar, Ace Executive Training Institute, 5000 Forbes Avenue, Pittsburgh, PA 15244. Ask that the seminar fees for three employees be returned because they cannot attend. Give yourself a title and supply any details necessary.

6.12 Direct Claim: A Matter of Mismeasurement

As the owner of Custom Designs, you recently completed a living room remodel that required double-glazed, made-to-order oak French doors. You ordered them, by telephone, on April 14 from Capitol Lumber and Hardware. When they arrived on May 18, your carpenter gave you the bad news: the doors were cut too small. Instead of measuring a total of 11 feet 8 inches, the doors measured 11 feet 4 inches. In your carpenter's words, "No way can I stretch those doors to fit these openings!" You waited nearly five weeks for these doors, and your clients wanted them installed immediately. Your carpenter said, "I can rebuild this opening for you, but I'm going to have to charge you for my time." His extra charge came to $376.

You feel that the people at Capitol Lumber should reimburse you for this amount because it was their error. In fact, you actually saved them a bundle of money by not returning the doors. You decide to write to Capitol Lumber and enclose a copy of your carpenter's bill. You wonder whether you should also include a copy of Capitol Lumber's invoice, even though it does not show the exact door measurements. You are a good customer of Capitol Lumber and Hardware, having used their quality doors, windows, and hardware on many other remodeling jobs. You're confident that it will grant this claim.

Your Task. Write a claim letter to Sal Rodriguez, Sales Manager, Capitol Lumber and Hardware, 3568 East Washington Avenue, Indianapolis, IN 46204.

6.13 Direct Claim: The Real Thing

Let's face it. Like most consumers, you've probably occasionally been unhappy with service or with products you have used.

Your Task. Select a product or service that has disappointed you. Write a claim letter requesting a refund, replacement, explanation, or whatever seems reasonable. Generally, such letters are addressed to customer service departments. For claims about food products, be sure to include bar-code identification from the package, if possible. Your instructor may ask you to actually mail this letter. Remember that smart companies want to know what their customers think, especially if a product could be improved. Give your ideas for improvement. When you receive a response, share it with your class.

WEB

6.14 Direct Reply: So You Want an Internship at the Gap?

The Gap Inc. headquarters in the San Francisco Bay area is a popular place to work. Many students inquire about summer internships. Although it supplies oodles of information about internships at its Web site, Gap Inc. still receives letters requesting this information. As one of its current summer interns, you have been given a task by your supervisor. She wants you to write a general letter that she can use to reply to requests from college students seeking summer internships. She doesn't have time to answer each one individually, and she doesn't want to tell them all to just go to the Web site. She feels responsible to reply in a way that builds goodwill for Gap, which also operates Old Navy and Banana Republic.

Your Task. Draft a reply to students seeking summer intern information. Go to the Gap Web site and study its offerings. Prepare a letter that describes the summer intern program, its requirements, and how to apply. Summarize some of the lengthy descriptions from the Web site. Use bulleted lists where appropriate. Since the letter may involve two pages, group similar information under side headings that improve its readability. Although your letter may become a form letter, address your draft to Lisa M. Hernandez, 493 Cesar Court, Walnut Creek, CA 94598.

WEB

6.15 Direct Reply: River Rafting on the Web

As the program chair for the campus Ski Club, you have been asked by the president to investigate river rafting. The Ski Club is an active organization, and its members want to schedule a summer activity. A majority favored rafting. Use a browser to search the Web for relevant information. Select five of the most promising Web sites offering rafting. If possible, print a copy of your findings.

Your Task. Summarize your findings in a letter to Brian Krauss, Ski Club president. The next meeting of the Ski Club is May 8, but you think it would be a good idea if you could discuss your findings with Brian before the meeting. Write to Brian Krauss, SIU Ski Club, 303 Founders Hall, Carbondale, IL 62901.

WEB

6.16 Direct Reply: Krispy Kreme Helps Raise Funds

Despite low-carb and low-fat diet fads, people still crave yummy doughnuts—especially the oh-so-light yet rich and scrumptious Krispy Kreme creations. As a customer service representative at Krispy Kreme in Winston-Salem, you have received a letter from a customer interested in using your doughnuts as a fund-raising activity for Noah's Ark Children's Center (see Activity 6.7). Although much of the information is at the Web site, you must answer this customer's letter personally.

Your Task. Respond to Mrs. Tiffany Lane, Noah's Ark Children's Center, 4359 Blue Creek Road, Austin, TX 78746. You need to explain the three ways that Krispy Kreme helps organizations raise funds. Use the Krispy Kreme Web site to gather information, but summarize and paraphrase what you find. Compose a letter that not only provides information but also promotes your product. Consider using bullet points and paragraph headings to set off the major points.

WEB

6.17 Direct Reply: What Is a FICO Credit Rating Score?

You were delighted to be selected as one of three interns for the prestigious architectural firm of Studio 1030. On the job you soon discovered that many of the firm's architects worked independently and relied on the office staff for clerical and technical support. One of the firm's retired architects, Harold M. Zimmerman, who lived in Benton Harbor, Michigan, was recently called back to the office because of the increasing demand for custom-designed homes. He was reluctant to return, saying that he's been out of touch. But Studio 1030 owner Lars Pedersen said, "Look, Hal, we really need you to help out for six months or so. We've got a support staff that will pitch in to assist you, if necessary."

Almost immediately, Mr. Zimmerman realized that the entire world of mortgage finance had changed in the past decade. He heard about two clients who were eager to have plans drawn for new homes, but they could not qualify for building loans because of low FICO scores. Mr. Zimmerman confessed to the owner that he knew very little about FICO at all. What's more, Mr. Zimmerman admitted that he was not comfortable doing Internet research.

The owner decides that this would be a good internship project for you. He asks you to prepare a letter to Mr. Zimmerman, who prefers to work at home, replying to his request for information about FICO. Although you've vaguely heard of it, you could not immediately define what the term means. However, you recognize a good opportunity when you see it! Here's a chance to learn something about credit ratings, and it's also a good chance to show off your research and communication skills.

Your Task. Go to *http://www.myfico.com* and study its information. (Use a search engine with the term "My Fico" if this URL fails.) What does "FICO" stand for? Who uses this term and why? What factors affect a FICO score? How can individuals improve their FICO scores? Summarize your findings in your own words in a well-organized, concise letter addressed to Mr. Harold Zimmerman, 2938 East Lakeview Avenue, Benton Harbor, MI 49022. Use bulleted lists for some of the information. Assume you are writing on Studio 1030 stationery.

INFOTRAC

6.18 Direct Reply: Restricting Internet Use on the Job

As an intern at a large accounting firm, you are surprised at the broad range of expertise expected of the CPAs. In fact, you think they may go too far in trying to please their clients. One client recently asked Greg Moltiere, your boss, to help her out with an Internet use policy for her small company. Although Mr. Moltiere is not an expert in this area, he wants to assist this client, who is not at all computer savvy. She has a growing company, and many of her employees are using the Internet. She called Mr. Moltiere and asked him to help her out with general information about Internet use policies. The client asked these questions: Why does a company need an Internet use policy? What does an Internet policy generally cover? Where can I see a sample Internet policy? Do I really need such a policy for my company?

Your Task. Mr. Moltiere asks you to use the Web to learn more about Internet use policies. For Greg Moltiere's signature, draft a direct reply letter answering the client's questions. His goal is to provide common information that encourages the client to develop an Internet policy for her company. Offer any additional material that you think will be useful. An InfoTrac search using the keywords "Internet Use Policy" will produce current information. Address the letter to Ms. Sherry Stratton, Stratton Convalescent Services, 2389 Three Rivers Boulevard, Poplar Bluff, MO 63901.

WEB

6.19 Direct Reply: Describing Your Major

A friend in a distant city is considering moving to your area for more education and training in your field. This individual wants to know about your program of study.

Your Task. Write a letter describing a program in your field (or any field you wish to describe). What courses must be taken? Toward what degree, certificate, or employment position does this program lead? Why did you choose it? Would you recommend this program to your friend? How long does it take? Add any information you feel would be helpful.

CRITICAL THINKING

6.20 Adjustment: A Matter of Mismeasurement

As Sal Rodriguez, sales manager of Capitol Lumber and Hardware, you must respond to a problem. Your firm manufactures quality precut and custom-built doors and frames. You have received a letter dated May 25 from Candace Olmstead (described in Activity 6.12). Ms. Olmstead is an interior designer, and she complains that the oak French doors she recently ordered for a client were made to the wrong dimensions.

Although they were the wrong size, she kept the doors and had them installed because her clients were without outside doors. However, her carpenter charged an extra $376 to install them. She claims that you should reimburse her for this amount, because your company was responsible for the error. You check her June 9 order and find that the order was filled correctly. In a telephone order, Ms. Olmstead requested doors that measured 11 feet 4 inches, and that's what you sent. Now she says that the doors should have been 11 feet 8 inches. Your policy forbids refunds or returns on custom orders. Yet, you remember that in the early part of June, you had two new people working the phones taking orders. It's possible that they did not hear or record the measurements correctly. You don't know whether to grant this claim or refuse it. But you do know that you must look into the training of telephone order takers and be sure that they verify all custom order measurements. It might also be a good idea to have your craftsmen call a second time to confirm custom measurements.

Ms. Olmstead is a successful interior designer and has provided Capitol Lumber and Hardware with a number of orders. You value her business but aren't sure how to respond.

Your Task. Decide how to treat this claim and then write to Candace Olmstead, Custom Designs, 903 Hazel Dell Parkway, Carmel, IN 46033. In your letter remind her that Capitol Lumber and Hardware has earned a reputation as the manufacturer of the finest wood doors and frames on the market. Your doors feature prime woods, and the craftsmanship is meticulous. The designs of your doors have won awards, and the engineering is ingenious. You have a new line of greenhouse windows that are available in three sizes. Include a brochure describing these windows.

6.21 Adjustment: Unhappy Customer Returns Desk

As Patrick Dwiggens, operations manager, Premier Wood Products, it is your job to reply to customer claims; and today you must respond to Valerie Vickers (described in Activity 6.10). You are disturbed that she is returning the executive desk (Invoice No. 3499), but your policy is to comply with customer wishes. If she doesn't want to keep the desk, you will certainly return the purchase price plus shipping charges. Desks are occasionally damaged in shipping, and this may explain the marred finish and the sticking drawers.

You will try to persuade Ms. Vickers to give Premier Wood Products another chance. After all, your office furniture and other wood products are made from the finest hand-selected woods by master artisans. Since she is apparently furnishing her office, send her another catalog and invite her to look at the traditional conference desk on page 10-E. This is available with a matching credenza, file cabinets, and accessories. She might be interested in your furniture-leasing plan, which can produce substantial savings.

Your Task. Write to Valerie Vickers, President, Financial Advisors, Inc., 203 Elm Street, Youngwood, PA 15697. In granting her claim, promise that you will personally examine any furniture she may order in the future.

6.22 Adjustment: No Birds Will Be Harmed

You didn't want to do it. But guests were complaining about the pigeons that roost on the Scottsdale Hilton's upper floors and tower. Pigeon droppings splattered sidewalks, furniture, and people. As the hotel manager, you had to take action. You called an exterminator, who recommended Avitrol. This drug, he promised, would disorient the birds, preventing them from finding their way back to the Hilton. The drugging, however, produced a result you didn't expect: pigeons began dying.

After a story hit the local newspapers, you began to receive complaints. The most vocal came from the Avian Affairs Coalition, a local bird-advocacy group. It said that the pigeons are really Mediterranean rock doves, the original "Dove of Peace" in European history and the same species the Bible said Noah originally released from his ark during the great flood. Activists claimed that Avitrol is a lethal drug causing birds, animals, and even people who ingest as little as 1/600th of a teaspoon to convulse and die lingering deaths of up to two hours.

Repulsed at the pigeon deaths and the bad publicity, you stopped the use of Avitrol immediately. You are now considering installing wires that offer a mild, nonlethal electrical shock. These wires, installed at the Maricopa County Jail in downtown Phoenix for $50,000, keep thousands of pigeons from alighting and could save $1 million in extermination and cleanup costs over the life of the building. You are also considering installing netting that forms a transparent barrier, sealing areas against entry by birds.

Your Task. Respond to Mrs. Deborah Leverette, 24 Canyon Lake Shore Drive, Spring Branch, TX 52319, a recent Scottsdale Hilton guest. She sent a letter condemning the pigeon poisoning and threatening to never return to the hotel unless it changed its policy. Try to regain the confidence of Mrs. Leverette and promote further business.[8]

6.23 Employment Recommendation: Recommending Yourself

You are about to leave your present job. When you ask your boss for a letter of recommendation, to your surprise he tells you to write it yourself and then have him sign it. Actually, this is not an unusual practice today. Many businesspeople find that employees are very perceptive and accurate when they evaluate themselves.

Your Task. Use specifics from a current or previous job. Describe your duties and skills. Be sure to support general characteristics with specific examples. In writing, speak of yourself in the third person (*Lisa worked under my supervision during the summer of . . . . Lisa was in charge of . . . . I consider her to be reliable . . .*).

6.24 Thanks for a Favor: Got the Job!

Congratulations! You completed your degree and got a terrific job in your field. One of your instructors was especially helpful to you when you were a student. This instructor also wrote an effective letter of recommendation that was instrumental in helping you obtain your job.

Your Task. Write a letter thanking your instructor.

TEAM

6.25 Thanks for a Favor: Emerging World of Online Networking

Your business communication class recently enjoyed a guest speaker, Diane Domeyer. She is executive director of OfficeTeam, the nation's leading staff service specializing in the temporary placement of highly skilled administrative and office support professionals. Her topic was "The Emerging World of Online Networking." At first, the class didn't know what online networking involved. Ms. Domeyer discussed special networks that allow individuals to network with others in their career fields at Web sites such as Ryze.com and ContactSpan.com. The International Association of Administrative Professionals even has a bulletin board in the Member's Place section of its Web site that allows members from around the world to connect. Your class learned about how to network online, including where to go, do's and don'ts, etiquette, and having realistic expectations.

Your Task. Individually or in groups, draft a thank-you letter to Ms. Diane Domeyer, Executive Director, Office Team, P.O. Box 310, Palo Alto, CA 94063. Use your imagination to fill in details.

6.26 Thanks for the Hospitality: Holiday Entertaining

You and other members of your staff or organization were entertained at an elegant dinner during the winter holiday season.

Your Task. Write a thank-you letter to your boss (supervisor, manager, vice president, president, or chief executive officer) or to the head of an organization to which you belong. Include specific details that will make your letter personal and sincere.

TEAM   WEB

6.27 Sending Good Wishes: Personalizing Group Greeting Cards

When a work colleague has a birthday, gets promoted, or retires, someone generally circulates a group greeting card. In the past it wasn't a big deal. Office colleagues just signed their names and passed the store-bought card along to others. But the current trend is toward personalization with witty, oh-so-clever quips. And that presents a problem. What should you say—or not say?

You know that people value special handwritten quips, but you realize that you're not particularly original and you don't have a store of "bon mots" (clever sayings, witticisms). You're tired of the old standbys, such as *This place won't be the same without you* and *You're only as old as you feel.*

Your Task. To be prepared for the next greeting card that lands on your desk at work, you decide to work with some friends to make a list of remarks appropriate for business occasions. Use the Web to research witty sayings appropriate for promotions, birthdays, births, weddings, illnesses, or personal losses. Use a search term such as "Birthday Sayings," "Retirement Quotes," or "Cool Sayings." You may decide to assign each category (birthday, retirement, promotion, and so forth) to a separate team. Submit the best sayings in a memo to your instructor.

6.28 Responding to Good Wishes: Saying Thank You

Your Task. Write a short note thanking a friend who sent you good wishes when you recently completed your degree.

6.29 Extending Sympathy: To a Spouse

Your Task. Imagine that a coworker was killed in an automobile accident. Write a letter of sympathy to his or her spouse.

VIDEO RESOURCES

Video Library 2, *Bridging the Gap*
Social Responsibility and Communication: Ben & Jerry's.
In an exciting inside look, you see managers discussing six factors that determine Ben & Jerry's continuing success. Toward the end of the video, you'll listen in on a discussion of a new packaging material made with unbleached paper. As a socially responsible company, Ben & Jerry's wanted to move away from ice cream packages made from bleached papers. Bleaching requires chlorine, a substance that contains dioxin, which is known to cause cancer, genetic and reproductive defects, and learning disabilities. In producing paper, pulp mills using chlorine are also adding to dioxin contamination of waterways. After much research, Ben & Jerry's found a chlorine-free, unbleached paperboard for its packages. That was the good news. The bad news is that the inside of the package is now brown.

Assume you've been hired at Ben & Jerry's to help answer incoming letters. Although you're fairly new, your boss gives you a letter from an unhappy customer. This customer opened a pint of Ben & Jerry's "World's Best

Vanilla" and then threw it out. After seeing the brown inner lid, he decided that his pint must have been used for chocolate before it was used for vanilla. Or, he said, "the entire pint has gone bad and somehow turned the sides brown." Whatever the reason, he wasn't taking any chances. He wants his money back.

Your Task. Write a letter that explains the brown carton, justifies the reason for using it, and retains the customer's business. Address the letter to Mr. Cecil Hamm, 1608 South McKenna, Poteau, OK 74954.

Video Library 2, *Bridging the Gap*
MeetingsAmerica. In Salt Lake City, MeetingsAmerica arranges conferences and conventions for visitors to the city. Businesses planning big conferences often outsource arrangements such as registration, ground transportation, special events, and other details. In this video you'll learn how MeetingsAmerica operates as a destination meeting organization. Your instructor may provide a special writing activity after you see this video.

GRAMMAR/MECHANICS CHECKUP—6

Commas 1

Review the Grammar Review section of the Grammar/Mechanics Handbook Sections 2.01–2.04. Then study each of the following statements and insert necessary commas. In the space provided write the number of commas that you add; write *0* if no commas are needed. Also record the number of the G/M principle illustrated. When you finish, compare your responses with those shown at the end of the book. If your answers differ, study carefully the principles shown in parentheses.

2 _____ (2.01) **Example**   Sometimes we are so engrossed in our job, our family, or a relationship that we forget about ourselves.

_____
_____
_____
_____
_____
_____
_____
_____
_____
_____
_____
_____
_____
_____

1. We think on the other hand that camera phones are not a good idea in offices.
2. We are certain Mr. Nosrati that your UPS delivery will arrive before 11 a.m.
3. Our software helps your employees be more creative collaborative and productive in team projects.
4. The spring leadership conference will take place April 3 at the South Beach Marriott Hotel beginning at 2 p.m.
5. Needless to say we were depressed at the stock market drop.
6. Amazon closed distribution centers in McDonough Georgia and Grand Forks North Dakota to save money.
7. By the way the best things in life aren't things.
8. The last council meeting that was recorded in the minutes was held on March 23 2005 in Phoenix.
9. Mr. Maslow Mrs. Kim and Ms. Garcia were all promoted.
10. The shipment addressed to McMahon Industries 6920 Main Street Detroit MI 48201 arrived two weeks late.
11. The manager feels nevertheless that the support of all employees is critical.
12. Successful teams encourage open communication resolve conflict fairly and promote interaction among members.
13. Our team works hard to retain your business Mr. Sherman.
14. President Carson however thinks that all staff members need training.
15. Rachel moved from Hartford Connecticut to San Diego California because she was offered a better job.

● GRAMMAR/MECHANICS CHALLENGE—6

The following letter has faults in grammar, punctuation, spelling, capitalization, number form, repetition, wordiness, and other problems. Correct the errors with standard proofreading marks (see Appendix B) or revise the message online at **Guffey Xtra!**

January 20, 200x

Mr. Jason R. Weingartner
3201 Rose Avenue
Mar Vista, CA 90066

Dear Mr. Weingartner:

SUBJECT: Your February 5th Letter Requesting Information About New All Natural
                     Products

We have received your letter of February 5 in which you inquire about our all-natural products. Needless to say, we are pleased to be able to answer in the affirmative. Yes, our new line of freeze dried back packing foods meet the needs of older adults and young people as well. You asked a number of questions, and here are answers to you're questions about our products.

- Our all natural foods contains no preservatives, sugars or additives. The inclosed list of dinner items tell what foods are cholesterol-, fat-, and salt-free.

- Large orders recieve a five percent discount when they're placed direct with Outfitters, Inc. You can also purchase our products at Malibu Sports Center, 19605 Pacific Coast Highway Malibu CA, 90265.

- Outfitters, Inc., food products are made in our sanitary kitchens which I personally supervise. The foods are flash froze in a patented vacum process that retain freshness, texture and taste.

- Outfitters, Inc., food products are made from choice ingredients that combines good taste and healful quality.

- Our foods stay fresh, and tasty for up to 18 months.

Mr. Weingartner I started Outfitters, Inc., five years ago because of the fact that discerning back packers rejected typical camping fare. Its a great pleasure to be able at this point in time to share my custom meals with back packers like you.

I hope you'll enjoy the enclosed sample meal, "Saturday Night on the Trail" is a four-coarse meal complete with fruit candys and elegant appetizers. Please call me personally at (213) 459-3342 to place an order, or to ask other questions about my backpacking food products.

Sincerely,

COMMUNICATION /\/\/\/WORKSHOP
CAREER SKILLS

DR. GUFFEY'S GUIDE TO BUSINESS ETIQUETTE
AND WORKPLACE MANNERS

Etiquette, civility, and goodwill efforts may seem out of place in today's fast-paced, high-tech offices. Yet, etiquette and courtesy are more important than ever if diverse employees are to be able to work cooperatively and maximize productivity and work-flow. Many organizations recognize that good manners are good for business. Some colleges and universities offer management programs that include a short course in manners. Companies are also conducting manners seminars for trainee and veteran managers. Why is politeness regaining legitimacy as a leadership tool? Primarily because courtesy works.

Good manners convey a positive image of an organization. People like to do business with people who show respect and treat others civilly. People also like to work in a pleasant environment. Considering how much time is spent at work, doesn't it make sense to prefer an agreeable environment to one that is rude and uncivil?

Etiquette is more about attitude than about formal rules of behavior. That attitude is a desire to show others consideration and respect. It includes a desire to make others feel comfortable. You don't have to become an etiquette nut, but you might need to polish your social competencies a little to be an effective businessperson today.

You can brush up your workplace etiquette skills online at your companion Web site *http://guffey.swlearning.com*. Look for "Dr. Guffey's Guide to Business Etiquette and Workplace Manners." Of interest to both workplace newcomers and veterans, this guide covers the following topics:

Professional Image	Business Cards
Introductions and Greetings	Dealing With Angry Customers
Networking Manners	Telephone Manners
General Workplace Manners	Cell Phone Etiquette
Coping With Cubicles	E-Mail Etiquette
Interacting With Superiors	Gender-Free Etiquette
Managers' Manners	Business Dining
Business Meetings	Avoiding Social Blunders When Abroad
Business Gifts	

To gauge your current level of knowledge of business etiquette, take the preview quiz at the student Web site. Then, study all 17 business etiquette topics. These easy-to-read topics are arranged in bulleted lists of Dos and Don'ts. After you complete this etiquette module, your instructor may test your comprehension by giving a series of posttests.

Career Application. You've been a manager at OfficeTemps, a company specializing in employment placement and human resources information, for a long time. But you've never received a letter like this before. A reporter preparing an article for a national news organization writes to you requesting information about how workplace etiquette is changing in today's high-tech environment. Her letter lists the following questions:

- Are etiquette and workplace manners still important in today's fast-paced Information Age work environment? Why or why not?
- Do today's workers need help in developing good business manners? Why or why not?
- Are the rules of office conduct changing? If so, how?
- What advice can you give about gender-free etiquette?

- What special manners do people working in shared workspaces need to observe?

The reporter asks for any other information you can share with her regarding her topic, "Information Age Etiquette."

Your Task
In teams or individually, prepare an information response letter addressed to Ms. Lindsey Ann Evans, National Press Association, 443 Riverside Drive, New York, NY 10024. Use the data you learned in this workshop. Conduct additional Web research if you wish. Remember that you will be quoted in her newspaper article, so make it interesting!

HOW TO WRITE ABOUT PROCESSES, INSTRUCTIONS, AND PROCEDURES

A process is a series of actions, changes, or functions that bring about a result. For example, the writing process results in a letter, memo, or report. A manufacturing process results in the production of a car. In this bonus supplement we're going to focus on how to write about processes, instructions, and procedures.

We're particularly interested in documenting processes in the workplace. You may find that your boss asks you to describe the hiring process so that every department can follow the same process. Or you may be asked to write a set of instructions for clearing the copy machine of jammed paper or installing new toner. You may be asked to prepare a set of instructions for using Word XP mail merge to create labels. Every business works with processes and instructions. In this bonus supplement you'll learn special techniques for describing processes and writing instructions. You'll also see a number of models to guide you as you apply what you have learned. But first let's review the three-part writing process, which is fully explained in Guffey's *Essentials of Business Communication* and *Business Communication: Process and Product*.

REVIEWING THE WRITING PROCESS

In any writing project, you can be more efficient and effective if you follow a step-by-step writing process. Whether preparing a memo, e-mail message, letter, report, or set of instructions, you will go through three phases: prewriting, writing, and revising.

Prewriting

Before writing, you need to analyze your purpose. What are you trying to accomplish? In writing about processes and instructions, you will probably decide that you want to write a set of instructions that is so clear that anyone could follow it without becoming confused. You also need to anticipate who will be reading your instructions. What does the audience already know about the subject? How much detail do you need to include? Do you need to define terms? How can you adapt this topic to the audience? If you were writing instructions for computer technicians, you could be fairly certain that they all understood the terms used. But if you were writing the same instructions for office personnel, you would have to use language they understood.

Writing

After deciding on your purpose and analyzing the audience, you will collect information. If you are writing about a process, you would be certain that you understood that process thoroughly. For example, if you were documenting a performance appraisal process for your company, you would probably talk with managers to learn how they do it. You might also check to see how other companies give such appraisals. You might search the Web to see whether any performance appraisal documents were available. When you had collected sufficient information, you would compose the first draft.

Revising

The final stage in the writing process involves editing, proofreading, and evaluating. This is the stage at which experienced writers spend the most time. They revise for clarity, conciseness, and vigor. They look at every sentence to be sure it can be understood. They also reorganize and find ways to highlight important information. Proofreading means reading to correct any grammar and mechanical problems. Finally, they evaluate the entire document to decide whether it accomplishes its purpose. In writing about processes and instructions, you might pilot test the document to learn whether its audience understands the concepts presented.

Comparing Processes and Instructions

As you learned earlier, a process is a series of actions, changes, or functions that bring about a result. In Hollywood the Academy of Motion Picture Arts and Sciences follows a specific process that leads to its Academy Awards. Nominations for the best picture award follow a process that governs eligible nominations and voting procedures. In business offices, managers follow a process for developing each year's budget. Computer technicians follow a process in installing printer drivers.

When we talk about processes, we need to distinguish between describing the process and giving instructions for performing the process. If your readers are to perform the process, you would write step-by-step instructions. If, however, your readers are to learn about the process and understand it, you would describe the process. Both processes and instructions are chronological; that is, they are developed in a sequence from the first step or stage to the final step or stage. You can see the difference between a process description and instructions in the following comparison. Notice that the process describes performance appraisals so that a reader can understand what is happening. The instructions, however, are written so that the reader knows what to do in conducting a performance appraisal.

Process Description	**Instructions**
The criteria to be used in the performance appraisal process should be reviewed. A conference room is reserved, and a time is selected that is convenient for both the employee and the supervisor. A meeting is arranged so that the appraisal form can be discussed.	Review the criteria to be used in performance appraisals. Reserve a conference room at a convenient time. Meet with the employee to discuss the appraisal form.

HOW TO DESCRIBE A PROCESS

Process description generally focuses on how something is done or made. How does a large company process thousands of incoming résumés? How is a slide show developed and run using PowerPoint? The goal is for the reader to understand the process, not perform the process.

To help you understand how to write about processes, we'll use the hiring process of the U.S. Border Patrol, shown in Figure 1, as an example.

Figure 1   Illustration of a Process

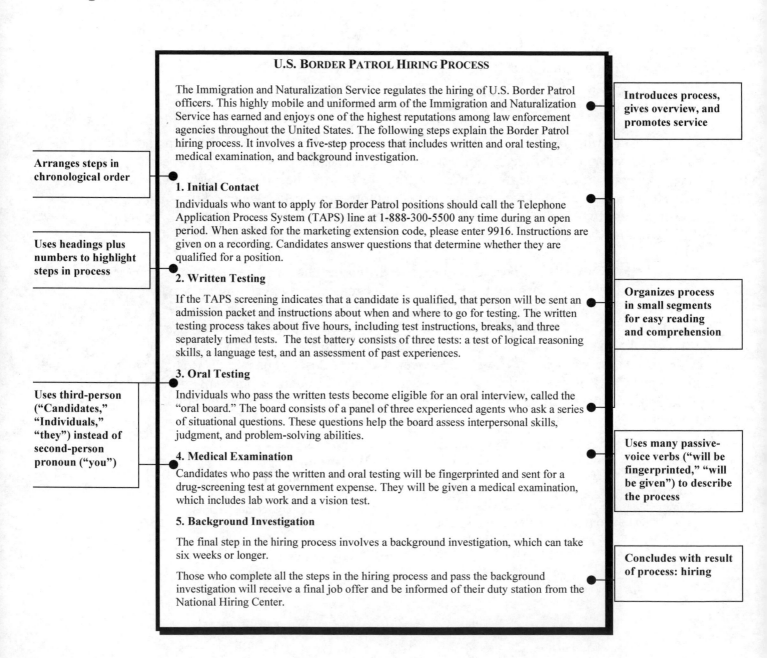

U.S. BORDER PATROL HIRING PROCESS

The Immigration and Naturalization Service regulates the hiring of U.S. Border Patrol officers. This highly mobile and uniformed arm of the Immigration and Naturalization Service has earned and enjoys one of the highest reputations among law enforcement agencies throughout the United States. The following steps explain the Border Patrol hiring process. It involves a five-step process that includes written and oral testing, medical examination, and background investigation.

Introduces process, gives overview, and promotes service

Arranges steps in chronological order

1. Initial Contact

Individuals who want to apply for Border Patrol positions should call the Telephone Application Process System (TAPS) line at 1-888-300-5500 any time during an open period. When asked for the marketing extension code, please enter 9916. Instructions are given on a recording. Candidates answer questions that determine whether they are qualified for a position.

Uses headings plus numbers to highlight steps in process

2. Written Testing

If the TAPS screening indicates that a candidate is qualified, that person will be sent an admission packet and instructions about when and where to go for testing. The written testing process takes about five hours, including test instructions, breaks, and three separately timed tests. The test battery consists of three tests: a test of logical reasoning skills, a language test, and an assessment of past experiences.

Organizes process in small segments for easy reading and comprehension

3. Oral Testing

Individuals who pass the written tests become eligible for an oral interview, called the "oral board." The board consists of a panel of three experienced agents who ask a series of situational questions. These questions help the board assess interpersonal skills, judgment, and problem-solving abilities.

Uses third-person ("Candidates," "Individuals," "they") instead of second-person pronoun ("you")

4. Medical Examination

Candidates who pass the written and oral testing will be fingerprinted and sent for a drug-screening test at government expense. They will be given a medical examination, which includes lab work and a vision test.

Uses many passive-voice verbs ("will be fingerprinted," "will be given") to describe the process

5. Background Investigation

The final step in the hiring process involves a background investigation, which can take six weeks or longer.

Those who complete all the steps in the hiring process and pass the background investigation will receive a final job offer and be informed of their duty station from the National Hiring Center.

Concludes with result of process: hiring

1. **Analyze the purpose and profile the audience.** The first task in describing a process is to define the purpose and profile the audience. Let's assume your job is to write a short summary of the hiring process for U.S. Border Patrol agents. This summary will appear at its Web site. You would begin by writing a purpose statement explaining what you aim to accomplish. For example, *The primary purpose of this process description is to present a brief summary to potential Border Patrol agents regarding the hiring process so that they will know what to expect. A secondary purpose is to encourage candidates to apply.* Although this purpose statement doesn't become part of your process document, it helps clarify your thinking. Next, you need to think about who will be reading this description. How much information will potential Border Patrol candidates need? How formal should you be? Should you use first-person pronouns (*I, we*), second-person pronouns (*you*), or third-person (*the candidate, they*)? Process descriptions, as illustrated in Figure 1, are often written in the third person.

2. **Collect information.** Writing about any process requires research. You need to talk with people who have performed or understand the process. You may use the Web to search for examples. In writing about the Border Patrol hiring process, you would probably consult people who do the testing and you would need to learn about the TAPS line described in the first step. You might want to call the number given to understand better what kind of telephone menu the caller hears. The important thing is to understand the process thoroughly so that you can write about it as an expert.

3. **Identify the main steps or segments in the process.** A process proceeds from a beginning to a conclusion. Your task is to clarify the steps in the process and separate them into meaningful segments. If possible, give them names. In the Border Patrol example, each of the five steps is named with an appropriate heading. Be sure that your headings are parallel. In Figure 1 notice that all of the headings are adjective-noun combinations.

4. **Select illustrations, if needed.** Some processes require illustration for readers to understand what's happening. These illustrations might take the form of pictures, symbols, icons, diagrams, organization charts, flow charts, or schematics. The hiring process for Border Patrol agents in Figure 1 required no illustrations. When you study the writing of instructions, however, you'll learn more about illustrations.

5. **Decide on the format.** Process descriptions may be short reports, written in manuscript form, such as that shown in Figure 1. But processes within business organizations may also be written as memos, e-mails, or letters. Figure 2 shows a process description included within an office memo.

Figure 2   Memo Describing a Process

TO: All Department Heads

FROM: Robert A. Hawkins, Vice President, Operations

DATE: Current

SUBJECT: CONDUCTING THE ANNUAL EQUIPMENT
               INVENTORY

At the request of CEO Edward Wiley, I am sending this memo reviewing the equipment inventory process for all departments. The primary reason for conducting this inventory is to determine what equipment is on hand and adjust our records accordingly. Here is the general process to be followed:

1. The annual inventory process begins October 2 each year. Each department will be given a copy of its inventory so that it can locate all items.

2. Each tag number should be checked against the actual equipment. Any changes or corrections must be noted.

3. Unlocated inventory should be reported. An explanation of what is believed to have happened to that equipment should be returned to the Property Office.

4. The completed inventory must be signed by the department head. That signature attests that a complete physical inventory has been completed and is correct.

5. All completed inventories should be returned to the Property Office by October 23. After completed inventories have been returned, the Property Office will compile a list of missing equipment and a second search will be conducted for those items.

We appreciate your cooperation in conducting an accurate inventory so that we know exactly what equipment is on hand.

Explains purpose for sending the memo

Arranges process in orderly steps

Uses many passive-voice verbs to describe process

nds with concluding atement that nticipates esult of process

6. Prepare an introduction. After you have developed the steps in the process, prepare an introduction. It should explain the topic, purpose, and intended audience as well as provide an overview of what follows.

7. Consider adding a conclusion. The last paragraph of a process document might summarize important points, discuss the result of the process, or include a concluding thought. Notice that the conclusion in the hiring process for Border Patrol agents explains the result of the process: hiring!

8. Revise and test the process. After writing the process, you'll want to read the entire document and revise it. Can it be better organized? Does it follow chronological order? Are the steps clearly identified? Could any sentences be stated more concisely? Is it grammatically and mechanically correct? A final step involves testing. It's always a good idea to have a potential reader examine the process and offer suggestions for making it easier to understand and implement.

HOW TO WRITE INSTRUCTIONS AND PROCEDURES

Thus far we've focused on writing process descriptions. Now let's turn to the writing of instructions (and procedures). Instructions show readers how to perform a task step by step. Well-written instructions enable readers to complete tasks consistently and efficiently. As a business communicator, you will probably be called on to write instructions at some point in your career. You may have to write instructions for employees to follow in making company travel reservations or reporting expenses. You may have to instruct employees in the operation of the voice mail system or how to back up computers. The following techniques can help you write effective workplace instructions.

1. Analyze the purpose and profile the audience. Before writing a set of instructions, ask yourself why you are writing the instructions. In Figure 3 an office manager wrote a simplified set of instructions for using the copy machine. The primary purpose was to instruct employees in efficient use. A secondary purpose was to remind employees that the copy machine was intended for work-related tasks only. When beginning to organize a set of instructions, write a statement of purpose, such as this: *The primary purpose of this set of instructions is to instruct employees in the proper use of the Canon XL20 copy machine. A secondary purpose is to remind employees that the copy machine is for work-related copies only.* Although the purpose statement does not become part of your instructions, it helps you focus on what you wish to accomplish. In the planning stages, you should also profile the audience. How much do they know about this process? What level of vocabulary is appropriate? When and where will they be using these instructions?

2. Identify the main steps and practice the task. Before describing a process, be sure that you have tried that process many times. To clarify the proper sequencing of steps, make a list of each step. Some people like to work backwards. What is to be done last, next to last, and so on? Why should the steps be done in the order you select? Watching a person performing the task for the first time can also be helpful. What was his or her very first action? Where and how did the person alter? What was the most difficult step? What steps will require the most ample instructions? Take full and careful notes.

Figure 3   Instructions for Operating Copy Machine

HOW TO OPERATE THE CANON XL20 COPY MACHINE

The Canon XL20 copy machine located in the Reprographics Department on the second floor may be used by any employee making work-related copies. If everyone follows these instructions and uses the machine carefully, we can reduce service costs and experience less downtime. Remember that this machine is for work copies only.

Loading Paper
1. Remove Paper Tray 1 by firmly pulling it backwards.
2. Select about 250 sheets of 8 ½ x 11-inch xerographic paper and align the edges of the sheets.
3. Insert the paper into the tray. Place the paper edges under the retaining clips.
4. Return the paper tray to its drawer.

Making Copies
1. Press the power switch to the "On" position. Wait for the flashing "Ready" indicator to stop flashing.
2. Place the original face down on the copyboard glass. Center it.
3. Set the number of copies desired by pressing the plus or minus button.
4. Press the "Start" button.

---

3. Decide whether you need definitions and a list of materials. Instructions with complex parts may need definitions and a parts list, such as that shown in Figure 4. Such a list identifies parts, materials, tools, or ingredients to assemble or recognize before beginning a task. If such a list is required, it should appear at the beginning of the set of instructions.

Figure 4 Illustration of Copy Machine Parts

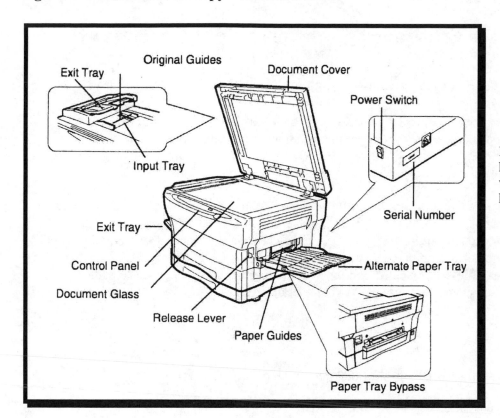

Instructions that tell consumers how to use a product often begin with a picture of the product that has all the parts clearly labeled.

4. Consider adding warnings or cautions. If any of the tasks are dangerous, warnings should appear before the step is taken or whenever an overlooked step might be risky. For example, a set of instructions explaining how to remove a floppy drive from a computer might include a warning to first discharge static electricity so that the inside of the PC is not damaged. A warning is often accompanied by a symbol, such as a triangle with an exclamation point inside:

⚠ **Warning! Turn off computer.**

5. Select illustrations, if helpful. Many "how-to" instructions use pictures, symbols, icons, and diagrams. Icons and symbols are useful for showing actions, and they can often replace words. Computer display screens use symbols such as ✂ to indicate "cut" and ▱ to indicate "e-mail." At the top of your computer screen, you'll see many symbols/icons to represent operations. Pictures and diagrams have the advantage of illustrating words or, in some instances, replacing words. Such illustrations reduce ambiguity, and they are particularly effective for readers who speak varying languages. Organization charts, flow charts, schematics, and screen captures simplify, clarify, and illustrate complex procedures. Notice in Figure 5 that computer screens help the reader understand the instructions for troubleshooting a problem.

Figure 5 Instructions With Computer Screen Illustrations

INSTRUCTIONS FOR DETERMINING THE IP ADDRESS OF A WINDOWS 2000 PROFESSIONAL CLIENT COMPUTER

Introduction

When a computer cannot connect to network resources, such as e-mail, computer technicians need to troubleshoot the problem. One connectivity problem involves improper configuration of a computer's IP address on the network. For example, if DHCP is down, a Windows 2000 Professional client will default to a 169.254.0.0 address and subsequently not be able to reach network resources outside its own subnet.

Even the simple transposition of two numbers in an IP address will cause the client to become isolated on the network. When this happens, a computer technician must be able to eliminate quickly the TCP/IP address of a client as the connectivity problem. To do this, the technician must open a command prompt and run the ipconfig command. This command displays the IP address of the client and also its subnet mask. From these two pieces of information, the computer technician can ensure that the IP address is properly configured for the client and then move on to other troubleshooting strategies to resolve the connectivity problem.

Process

1. Turn on the Windows 2000 Professional client. The desktop should be open.

2. Click the Start button at the bottom of the Start menu.

3. Click Run.

4. When the Run menu appears, type "cmd" in the "Open" box. Press Enter or click the OK button.

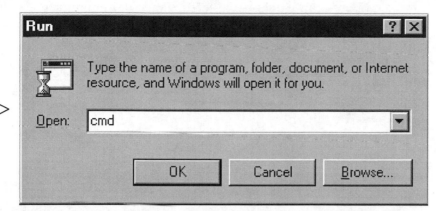

5. When the Command Prompt window appears, type "ipconfig." Press Enter.

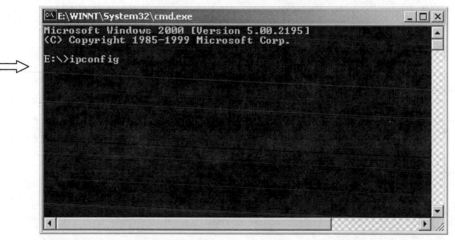

6. When the IP computer configuration displays, note that the IP address, subnet mask, and default gateway are identified. To keep this dialog box, press Alt + PrintScreen. Then open Word or WordPad, paste the dialog box into a document, and save or print it.

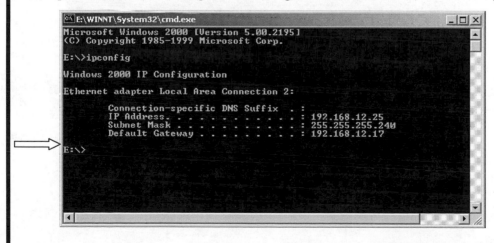

6. Decide on the format. The most readable sets of instructions generally appear in enumerated or bulleted lists. Typically, items are enumerated when a sequence of steps is being described. Items are bulleted when no special sequence is necessary. For example, a list of steps for using a copy machine would be numbered. But a list of safety tips for sending e-mail would be bulleted. Three common formats for instructions are shown in Figure 6. You might use Model 1 to describe guidelines for following an e-mail policy. Model 2 might be used for instructions on connecting an MP3 player to your computer. Model 3 format might be used for instructions on assembling an office style manual.

Figure 6   Three Formats for Instructions

Format 1 Model

Guidelines for _____

_____
_____

-   _____
-   _____
-   _____
-   _____
-   _____

This format is appropriate for establishing guidelines or rules, such as explaining a company's Internet or e-mail policy for employees.

Format 2 Model

How to _____

Introduction*

_____
_____

Materials Needed

_____ _____ _____
_____ _____ _____

Procedure*
1. _____
2. _____
3. _____
4. _____

*These sections are not always labeled.

This format is appropriate for explaining how to construct a product, such as assembling a bookcase or a bicycle.

Format 3 Model

Assembling a _____

_____
_____

[Diagram]

Definitions

_____ _____

_____ _____

Procedure
1. _____
2. _____
3. _____
4. _____

This format is appropriate for explaining how to install a product, such as mounting vertical blinds. It could also be used to describe the process surgeons use to scrub before surgery.

7. Make each step a separate command. How-to instructions are written in command mode (imperative mood). That is, each step begins with an active verb. For example, *Push the card into place* rather than *You should push the card into place.* Make sure each command is readable. Break up long sentences into shorter ones. The most readable sentences contain 17 or fewer words. Treat each step as a single, separate instruction. Retain the articles *a, an,* and *the* unless you do not have enough space. For example, *Press the arrow button* rather than *Press arrow button.* Place any necessary explanation after the step. For example, *Align the card in the slot. If the card is not seated firmly, the new hard drive won't work.*

8. Consider adding an introduction. Once you have outlined the steps in the process, write an introduction that explains the purpose and sets the scene for use of the instructions. Notice in Figures 3 and 5 that both sets of instructions begin with introductions that prepare the reader for the following steps.

9. Test and revise the instructions. Try the instructions out on several people who are unfamiliar with the procedures involved. You may find that some statements are confusing or out of sequence. Make adjustments based on the feedback you receive from your testers in the field.

LEARNING HOW TO WRITE INSTRUCTIONS ONLINE

You will find a colorful, interactive module that teaches you how to write instructions at the Guffey Web site <http://www.westwords.com/guffey/supplement_a.html>. [If this link is changed, look at the Guffey site index to locate Supplement A, "How to Write Instructions."]

Much of the material covered in this supplement is illustrated with hot links that take you to actual business Web sites. You can see how companies prepare instructions for their customers and employees. You'll also see how companies use organization charts, flow charts, and schematics. These online illustrations simplify, clarify, and illustrate complex procedures.

Be sure to check out the online module to help you comprehend, review, and retain techniques for writing about processes, instructions, and procedures.

ACTIVITIES AND CASES*

1. Using Command Language. Instructions are written as commands. Each step begins with an active verb.
Your Task. Convert the following statements into active voice and imperative mood.

Example: Common errors in typing and spelling can be automatically corrected by pressing AutoCorrect.
Revision: Press AutoCorrect to automatically correct common errors in typing and spelling.

a. Clip art can be inserted into documents by selecting an image and by clicking Open.

b. A hammer and a cold chisel should be used to chip away enough plaster to fully expose a wooden lath strip.

c. The flowers that you intend to dry should be picked about noon on a clear, dry day.

d. We expect you to speak from the podium and ample use of the microphone should be made.

e. A frozen plastic pipe should be wrapped with a towel and boiling water should be poured over it.

f. French-fried potatoes require that mature baking potatoes be cut into square sticks about 3/8 inch thick and then cold water should be used to soak them for 10 minutes.

g. Each guitar string must be tuned separately in order to match the pitch on a piano's note.

2. Résumé Writing: Brief Revision.
Your Task. Revise the following information into a brief list of instructions for preparing to write a résumé.
First, make a decision on a career goal. Then your background must be analyzed.
Next make a description of your education. Finally, you should list your work experience.

3. Team: Improving College Registration Instructions. The Director of Admissions at your institution asks a group of student workers to help him revise the admission and registration instructions. He's heard complaints that the present instructions are unclear.
Your Task. Look up the admission procedure in your class schedule or catalog. Write an improved version, including a title. Submit it to your instructor.

4. Revising Instructions for Imported Fax Machine. The following instructions came with a new imported fax machine, the TurboFax 3200. All the employees in your office are eager to use the machine, but they can't understand the instructions.

*Instructors: Proposed solutions are available at the Guffey Instructors Web site.

Your Task. Write improved instructions that include a reminder that this machine is intended for office work only. Submit your instructions to your instructor.

For Transmission. Document is facing down for loading. Document guides adjusted to document width. Operator is inserting the leading butt of document into feeding slot. [With sheets of two or more pages, leading edges are forming a slope as the operator lightly inserts them into feeding position; bottom sheet is proceeding first.] Operator is then picking up telephone handset. With continuous dial tone, dialing other fax number. Other fax's answering tone signals. Operator is pressing START key. When start lamp twinkles on-off, operator is hanging up handset.

5. Instructions for Car Emergencies. The Automobile Club wants to produce a short set of instructions to help motorists when their cars break down.
Your Task. Use the following information to write a logical set of instructions. Be sure to give your instructions a title.

You can protect yourself and your motor vehicle if you follow these suggestions. Your four-way flashers should be turned on. If your vehicle breaks down on a highway, don't just leave it where it stops. Positioning it as far as possible from the roadway is safest. The hood of the vehicle should be opened. When you get out, the passenger side is the best way to leave. To indicate distress, you should attach a light colored cloth to the antenna. If your vehicle has no antenna, use the door handle. It's a good idea to stay with your vehicle until uniformed law enforcement arrives.

Warning: You should beware of individuals in civilian clothes who are driving unmarked cars, even if they show what appears to be a law enforcement badge. You should not roll down your windows or get out of your vehicle for anything other than a marked law enforcement vehicle. If a person approaches, a window may be rolled down slightly and a request made for the person to call law enforcement.

If you must walk, think about leaving a note in your vehicle. It should contain your name, the date, the time that you left, and the direction in which you headed. If you accept a ride with another motorist, do the same thing. Write a note but also include the name of the person giving the ride and that person's license plate number.

6. Web Search: How to Buy a Computer. You have been asked to present a Brown-Bag Lunchtime talk for your employee association on the topic of buying a computer. You would like to distribute a simple handout with step-by-step instructions on how to do this.
Your Task. Use your favorite search tool (such as <www.google.com>) with the following search term: "how to" buy computer. Ignore all the sites that are selling computers, books, hardware, and software. Find those that actually provide guidance for purchasers. Using the techniques you learned in this chapter, prepare a list of instructions with no more than ten steps. Be sure to include a title and introduction. If you prefer not to give your talk on buying a computer, you could describe how to buy a car online or how to buy a used car. Web research will provide information on all of these topics.

7. Describing a Process: Campus Computer Loan Program. As a student intern in the dean's office of your college, you have been asked to draft a memo to department heads describing the process for low-interest loans to parents of students who want to purchase a Dell computer. The process begins at the College Computing Center where students may choose a Dell computer system. Then a loan promissory note is mailed to the parent/guardian. But the Business Office must first approve the loan application. If students have questions about the loan process, they should call Shirley Davis in the Business Office. The loan promissory note must be signed by the parent/guardian and returned along with a down payment to the Business Office. Loans are made for up to 24 months at a 5 percent interest rate. The down payment is at least 10 percent. There is a $100 processing fee and a $50 shipping/handling fee. Payments by credit card are not accepted. Once all the terms are confirmed, the Computing Center orders the computer and notifies the borrower when the shipment arrives.

Your Task. For the signature of Dean F. T. Wall, prepare a memo that describes the process concisely. The memo will be sent to students and parents who inquire. Add any details you think are necessary.

8. Computer Instructions: How to Share a Local Printer. Before a local print device can be used by other users on a network, it must be added to a computer on the network. Starting with Windows 95 and through Microsoft's latest version of the local client (Windows 2000 Professional), users have used the Start/Settings/Printers/Add Printer sequence to install the print drivers that allow the local computer to communicate with the attached local printer. This process is not difficult and depends only on the user's having the correct printer driver or knowing where to find the correct printer driver on the Internet. Let's assume that you have an HP LaserJet4 printer, and the drivers have already been installed.

Your Task. Prepare a set of instructions explaining how to share the HP LaserJet4 printer so that other users on the network can print to it. These instructions will be given to employees in a training class where they are learning to troubleshoot problems. Choose a specific Microsoft Client (Windows 95, Windows 98, Windows Millennium, Windows NT 4.0 Workstation, or Windows 2000 Professional). Write the process so that someone unfamiliar with the reason printers are shared will understand why this is an important part of networking. Make sure the steps are clearly defined and supported with screen shots. Use Alt + Print Screen to capture dialog boxes. Use the "paint" feature to modify screen shots, and use "tables" to make the document look professional. Your instructions should be similar to those shown in Figure 5. Include an introduction that explains the purpose and reason for the instructions.*

9. Additional Activities. Your instructor may select one or more of the following activities for you to write about:
a. How to back up computer files
b. How to format and partition a hard drive
c. How to look for a job online
d. How to organize department e-mails
e. How to track copies made on an office copier
f. Describe how a voice mail system works
g. Describe a loan application process
h. Describe how to develop and run a PowerPoint slide show
i. Describe the process of planning a conference

*Special thanks to Kevin Carpenter, Heald College, for providing this activity and its solution.